Be Your Own Harmonist

Be Your Own Harmonist

Awakening Your Inner Wisdom for Physical,
Mental, and Emotional Well-being

Lola Till

Waterside Productions

Gratitude to publisher Sounds True, Inc. for permission to excerpt
from Chakra Meditation © 2012 by Layne Redmond.

Printed in the United States of America

First Printing, 2020

ISBN-13: 978-1-949001-77-8 print edition
ISBN-13: 978-1-949001-78-5 eBook edition

Waterside Productions
2055 Oxford Ave
Cardiff, CA 92007
www.waterside.com

This book is dedicated to all those searching for strength in these extraordinarily challenging times. My hope is that it might provide sustenance needed as we work together to build a more harmonious world.

If you can detach yourself from all worldly worries,
You will live in the rapture of Eternity's garden.
If you purify yourself with the holy water of abstinence,
The murkiness of your heart will change into clear light.
If you can separate yourself from the house of desires,
You will come into the sanctuary of Divine Majesty.
In the heart of the ocean of Unity, you're not
A pearl that any worldly money can buy;
If you are brave enough not to grovel in the dust,
You can find a home in the heights of heaven.
If you dive now headfirst into profound contemplation,
You can dissolve all the past debts of destiny.
Doing such things are the sign of the real seeker–
The sign of fire of those who race along the Path.

– Rumi

Contents

Preface.. ix

Introduction.. xvii

Author's Note.. xxiii

Part One

Our Physical Body & the Abdominal Energy Center......................... 1

Chapter 1

Life in Our Bodies: Cells & Microorganisms............................... 7

Chapter 2

Sweet Enemies, Chronic Inflammation & Fasting....................... 13

Chapter 3

The Truth about Calories... 19

Chapter 4

The "Food" Industry.. 23

Chapter 5

Vegan: To Be, or Not to Be... 25

Chapter 6

A Balanced Daily Diet & High-Frequency Food......................... 45

Chapter 7

The Gluten-Free Diet Myth... 53

Chapter 8

Life after I Quit Caffeine & Alcohol.. 57

Chapter 9

Better Sleep, Better Life: Deep Sleep, Its Benefits & Tips on How to
Achieve It... 65

Chapter 10

Fascia & Yoga: New Importance for an Ancient Practice............ 71

Part One Conclusion... 75

Part Two

The Mental Energy Center... 79

Chapter 11

Modern Challenges.. 83

Chapter 12

Brain Waves & Why They Matter... 87

Chapter 13

Neuroplasticity & Good Mental Habits... 95

Chapter 14

Meditation for Brain Fitness... 99

Chapter 15

The Power of the Self-Healing Breath.. 103

Chapter 16

Do One Thing at a Time... 109

Part Two Conclusion... 115

Part Three

The Emotional Energy Center... 119

Chapter 17

Your Heart Intelligence Is More Powerful Than Your Brain Intelligence...... 125

Chapter 18

Be Your Best Friend: Practical Ways to Enhance Your Resilience.............. 129

Chapter 19

Forgiveness, Hawaiian Style... 135

Chapter 20

Letting Go of Emotional Pain: A Personal Story................................. 139

Chapter 21

The Health of Our Planet: A Reflection of the Health of Our Modern

Society.. 147

Conclusion: Your Limitless & Eternal Nature.................................... 157

Notes... 166

Bibliography... 176

Reviews.. 186

About the Author.. 188

Preface

"Knowing yourself is the beginning of all wisdom."
— Aristotle

Various forms of self-identification in society change over time. They reflect a person's national and cultural heritage. Navajo nation, for example, introduce themselves by the names of their parents and grandparents. You even sometimes hear people identified, behind their backs, by the size of their bank account or their net worth, and honorary titles are still important in Europe. As silly as it sounds, society also assesses people by how many social media followers and likes they have.

I won't be talking about my followers and likes here, or taking a deep dive into my ancestry, because they're only mental constructs. Those labels society assigns to us serve no purpose other than to separate us, to divide us into national, cultural, religious, and demographic categories. Associating ourselves and each other with different mental constructs about who we think we are takes away our fundamental right to be free and to experience our fullest potential.

Instead, the purpose of this book is to push all of those secondary categories and labels away and tell you about *yourself*. I don't take credit for any of the philosophies, discoveries, and facts presented in these pages; the truth has always been here for those who search for it. Rather, my intention is to showcase some of those long-known truths and share the latest scientific research and some other knowledge I've accumulated over the years.

Since I was a child, I've been searching for answers to core questions about myself, particularly those involving the indelible connection between body and soul. Some of the answers I've found are based in science, others in spirituality. But the future of human progress lies in the merging of science and spirituality, since one cannot be separated from the other.

This book offers you much necessary theoretical and practical information to lead you to both a physically healthy body and a vigorous spirit and, as a result, to both inner freedom and peace of mind. You'll learn how to maintain space within yourself so that you can experience the beauty of your humanness on many different levels. This is especially important because we create so much noise in our lives through our actions, thoughts, and emotions to the extent that we eventually cease enjoying the sacred gift of being alive.

Since ancient times, many wise thinkers have pondered the meaning of human existence, happiness, freedom, and destiny. Countless works have been written on these subjects and millions of opinions expressed, all of them essentially derivative of, and secondary to, the central question: "Who am I?"

That question has been clearly, deeply resonating inside me since childhood and has propelled me down a path of exploration in search of inner freedom, peace, understanding of the world around me, and of the healing needed for some of my serious health problems. This book is the sum total of what I've come to know, and what I would like to share with you, hoping that what has helped me might help you, too.

I'm a little over forty years old. I've taken in and processed a huge amount of information, checked it against my personal experiences and the experiences of close friends and acquaintances, and learned that this awareness has the power to change habits and thinking processes.

"Who am I?" a question as timeless as humankind itself and one I imagine you've asked yourself often, can be answered with:

You are the Consciousness embodied. You are a pure being, without limits, without age, without death. You are the being that experiences the entire universe while simultaneously containing the whole universe within yourself. Because you're aware, you can hear with your ears and see with your eyes; you can feel with your skin and smell with your nose.

You are eternally free, and your true nature never changes. Changes only occur in the things you experience: your body, your thoughts, and your emotions. For example, remember when you were a child and contrast that image with yourself as an adult now. Your body is no longer the same, but it's the same you. You constantly experience a kaleidoscope of emotions and values. "Yesterday I was angry, but now I'm happy." "Once, I had a certain point of view, but now I think differently." You operate simultaneously on physical, mental, and emotional levels, but it's still the same *you*.

Yet, we can lose sight of our true selves as we get caught in the web of our daily lives that then interferes with our natural balance. We mistake our emotions and experiences for our essences, and we associate ourselves with our moods so closely that in difficult moments, we forget our sense of the present moment.

We're so absorbed by our problems and thoughts that we no longer see the space, the difference, between them and our true selves. Our thoughts often lead to stress and dissatisfaction. The physical or mental pain we experience doesn't allow us to find harmony in ourselves and feel the Being of our authentic nature. We lose ourselves, and the vital connection to our Source.

This book explains how we can restore that balance between body, mind, and soul and lead us back to rediscovering our natural eternal beingness.

After received my master's degree in international law from the University of World Economy and Diplomacy in Tashkent, Uzbekistan, I realized that being a lawyer was not really my calling; so I went on to study for a doctorate degree in psychology at Tashkent State University. Just after I left school, I began volunteering at an Uzbekistan orphanage. I was so moved by the pain in those children's eyes, by the suffering and all the complications they had to put up with at such a young age, that I vowed to set up a charitable organization to help them. A few years later, when I was twenty-four, I founded the You Are Not Alone Foundation, a philanthropy dedicated to improving the lives of orphaned and abandoned children in Uzbekistan.

We began our work by setting up a legal department that helped children who'd been wrongly ejected from orphanages, and helped other ones reclaim housing that was rightfully theirs. Without parents or tutors, many of these children didn't have the chance to continue their schooling, so we also set up a learning center where we worked with teachers to prepare them for higher education. Then we expanded the foundation's work to help children with special needs in the areas of diagnoses, therapy, and education. I recently extended my charitable work to include educational programs aimed at offering scholarships to young Uzbekistanians to help them pursue their postgraduate studies at various European universities.

From 2008 to 2018, I lived between Geneva and Paris serving as Uzbekistan's ambassador to the United Nations Educational, Scientific, and Cultural Organization (UNESCO). I've since stepped down from that position to devote more time to research into better understanding human nature, behavior, and overall well-being, including studying the energy structure of food and traditional herbal healing.

I was born in a country that no longer exists. I was just a girl when Uzbekistan declared its independence from the Soviet Union. I still remember that time very well, especially how the fantasy of the promised communist utopia shattered after the music, films, and all kinds of other Western influences came bursting in. I will also always remember my first trip to the United States at age fourteen when I learned the valuable lesson that our own experience is far more credible than what's imposed on us by others.

The Uzbek city in which I grew up became the capital of a new state after the collapse of the Iron Curtain. It was bright and architecturally fascinating, reflecting its history as a landmark on the Silk Road, a trade route for Marco Polo and other merchants who brought fine spices and silks from China to a variety of European and Middle Eastern destinations. As a result, I was raised in a multinational, multicultural environment that had a profound impact on me, and continues to.

Behind the closed doors of our family residence, I was raised in an intense household with busy, prominent parents and a sister with whom, to put it politely, I have never established any closeness with at all. I look back on my childhood as an isolated one, having lived in a big house where it seemed as if no one else was around. I found great comfort from companionship with my dog, and from the serenity of our large property blessed with its natural beauty. To this day, I'm happiest and most connected to myself and to my life when I'm surrounded by nature.

Besides my pets and natural surroundings back then, my other favorite companion was our incredible library filled with so many books. Despite widespread shortages at the time, my father's influential government position allowed him access to every book imaginable from libraries in Moscow; from children's literature to international collections of philosophical, religious, biographical, and cultural works. I learned to read at a very early age, and became almost addicted to books with so much curiosity that I was always trying to find my way and wondering where and how I could fit in. The more I read over the years, the more I learned, and the more I learned, the more I wanted to learn; that pattern continues to this day. From those countless books, independent research, wonderful teachers, and life itself, I've been blessed with a wealth of insights and spiritual awakenings that have helped me grow into the grateful, healthy, happily married mother of three that I am.

I understand that the story of my life is not ordinary. It is somewhat reminiscent of Oriental tales of masters, princesses, power, good and evil, loyalty and betrayal. My destiny was to be born into the family of the first president of Uzbekistan. I was called a princess but absolutely did not feel like one.

Each of us has our own personal history that makes us who we are. What's happened to us since our birth is reflected in our thoughts, habits, and deeds. It is essential for our physical and mental health to look at our own lives with emotional distance and realize all that has happened and is happening to us are merely components of our creation as whole beings.

Realizing this, and fully accepting your past, can bring peace to your soul so that your personal history is no longer important to you. By letting it go, you release a huge amount of energy to be available for the present moment, the here and now, the most important moment in your life, the moment when you are exactly who you are.

I encourage you to let go of preconceptions and mental constructs about yourself and about other people so that nothing will affect your clarity. If you would like to understand the laws your body obeys; how to be your own best friend; how to help yourself physically, mentally and emotionally; how to experience life's turbulence while remaining in the center of its existence; and how to not succumb to the negative influence of external factors, then take my hand.

Introduction

We live in a world brimming with unimaginable innovations and break-throughs, but still we do not really have a clue about what the world is made of. Leading-edge scientists across the globe dedicate themselves to dividing particles into smaller and smaller sections known as quarks, and studying their properties, but still we have not gotten a hold on where they come from. Not even close. In fact, it is one of the universe's greatest mysteries.

There is a belief, more widely held across the globe than one might think, that the commonality among all objects is a kind of consciousness field, rather than a physical material one. Similarly, there is a theory in some philosophical communities that matter itself may well be an illusion—this is a notion we must dispel with as much certainty just as we wake ourselves from bad dreams.

Nevertheless, we have become obsessed with objectivity. We latch on to "thing-ness." We resonate with our bodies, thoughts, and yearnings and come to associate and identify with things, sometimes even solely with them. We let our minds and hearts skip hyper-consciously between our desires and drives so much that I can't help but wonder: Do these movements truly define us, or do we exist beyond form and frame?

Imagine the world as a giant screen. In this metaphor, each person is only a single pixel. Pixels, by nature, are only a part of the entire image they depict. They can only impersonally bind with the other pixels. Each, if it could sense, would see how different she is from those around her, and not realize that essentially every bit of the screen would be almost exactly alike, just as every water droplet is imbued with many of the same qualities as the sea itself. Any difference pales in comparison to their sameness. And at the end of the day, it is their sameness that is striking and whole.

So too, perhaps, we acknowledge that we can feel and understand suffering even if it is not happening directly to us. Not only do I believe in this connectedness and its power to bind us together, I also believe it is the secret to empowered evolution. I believe that surrendering to communality can guide each of us to a more peaceful, joyful world, and to a more peaceful, joyful self.

You see, every human is imbued with source energy, spark, godliness. To an extent, we all feel it as the pure, unabashed liveliness, almost foolishness, of our inner child. How can we get closer to this most sacred vibe? How can we follow in the footsteps of the ancient poet Rumi and let love be our cure? If we are to pull the future toward us in the most hopeful and egalitarian way, we must listen closer, we must dig deeper, we must not stop until we reach the core of our beingness. So, come along on this journey in three parts: body, mind, and soul.

The Body

The foods and drinks we consume have vibrations. I'll outline in an upcoming chapter a nutritional approach that has enabled me to discover, after twenty-five years of exploration and study, my own definition of overall wellness. If we are self-aware, distortions in our fields can be diagnosed before they appear in our bodies. We can become detectives of our own physical states, and can heal and grow strong through the way we fuel ourselves. Since our bodies are vessels to explore the universe, we might as well embolden them to be as powerful and glorious as possible. I see this as a privilege.

The Mind

Sensors inside us work to deliver information loudly and clearly. But sometimes this information can be limited, glitchy, or even harmful. More to the point, our minds belong to us; we do not belong to them. Each of us deserves to understand our own north star and live according to our most accurate, exciting compass. Understanding neuroplasticity, and also neural rewiring through breathing and meditating, offers an opportunity to expand our viewpoints and find our inner truths.

The Heart

Our third and final focus is arguably the most important: the soul, the heart, the emotional cradle. The subject of the soul has been, and continues to be, treated with intense and tender reverence throughout different cultures and throughout humankind. Together, we will unpack a most brilliant invention, learn to navigate feelings, and maintain emotional health even amidst daily obstacles and turmoil. Everything you see around you, everything that happens to you, is a reflection of what your heart perceives. Yes, our hearts can be blocked by simple triggers. But they can also be unblocked with training.

When our hearts are cut off, we are cut off from the good stuff. When our brains are cut off, we are cut off from the good stuff. When our bodies are cut off, we are cut off from the good stuff. Indeed, all three activation centers are bound together, and it is only in synchronicity when they allow us to access the ways of prophecy and ecstasy.

In addition to our physical bodies, we also have different energetic layers that vibrate across various ranges. For example, our physical bodies vibrate in lower ranges than are perceptible by our sensors. Each person's center—the physical, energetic, mental and emotional—generates its own vibrations. The vibrations of your physical body depend on the vibrations of its cells, organs, and foods you consume. However, your sensors only work within a limited range, which means that many things are hidden.

For example, vibrations of the mental, emotional, and energetic centers are not visible to the naked eye. Physical body health depends on energy flows. Mental center health depends on the thoughts and focuses of our attention. And the emotional center depends on the emotions in which we most often reside. Together, this combination creates an overall vibration with all of the centers being responsive to one another, for better or for worse. The higher our vibrational range, the higher our quality of life, and vice versa.

Thus, you can affect all the centers by fixing any one of them. We'll discuss various approaches to do this in upcoming chapters.

When our bodies are out of order and we experience health problems, or when our emotions or bad thoughts disturb us, we tend to focus on them and not on our lives or who we really are. We often mistake our bodies for our true and infinite nature, thinking, "I am this body," or "I am this personality or character." Those are shells no more "us" than our clothing is, and in reality, are only called upon as backup to help us toward a realization of who we are.

Without understanding our true nature, we're vulnerable to turbulence caused by our own wrong choices and behaviors, all of which emanate from our weak bodies, negative thoughts, and disempowering emotions. Instead, by understanding that quality of life depends on our health, we realize that our bodies are mortal, but our essence is immortal. This book is dedicated to that exact premise.

Once you realize who you really are, I believe your commitment to collective spirit and peace will naturally find its wings and fly. Because only when we find our own unique power will we find our own true connection, true love, true existence, in its most simple, earthy, and holy form.

The ultimate duality is this: we must not take ourselves too seriously, but we also must not take our magic too frivolously. When we act with this in mind, the possibilities for what we can do are truly infinite.

Author's Note

"If you want to find the secrets of the universe, think in terms of energy, frequency and vibration."
— Nikola Tesla

At some stage in its development, human civilization came to understand that the material world is not the only world, perhaps not even the most important world. There is a more subtle plan in the universe, primary and decisive. It isn't an artificial principle, it's a universal law—a powerful, omnipresent energy acknowledged in many cultures by different names. In Taoism, they call it *qi* or *ki*. In Buddhism and Hinduism, they call it *prana*.

Even modern scientists, who are notoriously skeptical of the unseen, are beginning to agree that matter is just a form of the expression of energy. In 1935, Dr. Harold Barr, a renowned professor of neuroanatomy at Yale University, confirmed the existence of an "energy envelope." He discovered that all living things are surrounded by an energy, or pranic body, and that this pranic body, which he called the electrodynamic field, regulates the functions of the physical body and controls the growth, shape, and destruction of cells, structures, and organs. Further Yale research found a direct connection between the mind and this electrodynamic field—for example, any mental imbalance has an impact on the field.

According to Chinese cosmology, in the beginning, there was a void, and out of this void sprang forth the duality of feminine and masculine energies: yin and yang (or, biblically, Adam and Eve). These energies are two opposing but complementary forces, with Yang representing Heaven, the Father, and the Creative, and yin representing Earth, the Mother and the Receptive. Yin and yang are dependent on one another, meaning that both are required for the universe to exist, and that we cannot know one without the other. How would we know "light," for instance, if we did not know "dark"?

Resonance in the relationship between humanity and nature is supremely important. The microcosm (humanity) is a reflection of the macrocosm (the universe). The energy of the Heavens (yang) is said to flow down to the Earth (yin), which collects it and returns it, forming humanity and all of life to create the Cosmic Trinity of Heaven, Humanity, and Earth. There is nothing mystical or esoteric about this energy at the core of everything in the Universe, and at the core of our bodies. It governs everything from our physical health to our thoughts, emotions, and spiritual experiences. It infuses the tiniest subatomic particles we're made of, which are in constant flux and motion. That motion translates into the energy that animates our bodies. As part of this energy system, it is our sacred duty to be graciously respectful of what gives us life, and to maintain integrity with all we create and destroy.

Albert Einstein observed that our bodies are slowed-down versions of energy, which explains why we can see our bodies and touch them, unlike thoughts, for example, which have a higher frequency and are therefore invisible and intangible. So, the energy in our bodies is an essential but often overlooked factor in our quest for our greatest, most complete well-being.

We can interpret a person to be an energy field with several distinct levels which influence and complement each other. The visible one is the physical body. The rest we call the aura. Each level of an aura has a different frequency. Some of these levels connect with our emotions and thoughts and create new qualities.

The first is the energetic level, which collects and distributes energy from points known as chakras. Various chakras relate to different levels of the aura and vibrate at different frequencies, with sensitives that are able to perceive forms in different colors.

The aura encompasses all levels of consciousness. It's governed by our immortal soul, our Higher Self—the goal of any life is to realize and embrace its Higher Self. Diseases in our bodies are manifestations of a distortion of frequencies within or between different levels of the aura and Higher Self; and most modern diseases originate at the mental level (from distorted thinking and from a distorted understanding of life and its laws) and at the emotional level (from destructive emotions such as self-pity, judgment, guilt, and hatred). If our physical body is not healthy, if we're anxious or depressed, if our thoughts are out of control and taking us to the darkest of places, we are too far away from the realization of our Higher Nature, too far away from achieving peace and harmony.

This book is an adapted version of the ancient concept of the three main energy centers in our bodies, how to attune and balance them to become healthy, and thus how to find the meaningful, peaceful lives we were born to live. The information in the following chapters will guide you to an awakening of your energy centers. Over time, the awakening of one center will trigger a chain of events to awaken the others. It can happen through your physical center, mental center, or emotional center, but wherever the awakening begins it will ultimately lead you to the realization of your True Nature.

Our three energy centers are also called our Inner Suns—we depend on the sun, after all, to give life to all living things. When these three energy centers, our body, mind, and soul, are functioning correctly and are aligned with each other, when there's unity among them, we enjoy health and the realization of our highest nature.

The first Sun, or energy center, located between and just above our eyebrows, is connected to the mental body. The second Sun is located in the heart region and is connected to the emotional body. The third Sun, in the mid-torso area two fingers above the navel, is connected to the physical body. Unblocked and in harmony with each other, these three Suns receive energy from the Earth/Yin, which freely rises to our centers from the bottom (lower center) to the top (upper center); and in turn, the energy of Heaven/Yang is received, moving to the centers in our bodies from the top to the bottom.

Sadly, life today makes it more challenging than ever to maintain harmony between our three Suns. External distractions have overloaded them and thrown them off balance. Our imbalanced abdominal energy, which corresponds directly with our physical body, has become obsessed with humanity's latest dysfunction: overconsumption from consuming tastier, chemically enhanced foods we think we need to the mindless consumption of things we know we don't need but still want. This is a condition that I'm recovering from myself.

Our mental Sun is being flooded with a nonstop barrage of information, some of it important but most of it trivial, that we have to continually process. And then there are our preoccupations with anxiety and pressure to spend every moment of every day being busy multitasking and striving to do everything right *now*. Our emotional Sun is suffering from a social-media-triggered dependence on universal approval at the expense of the pleasure of live communication and personal, face-to-face connections. By restoring maximum health and harmony to our mental, emotional, and physical energy bodies and thereby reigniting the three inner Suns that shine in each of us, it opens opportunities to live to our greatest potential.

PART 1

OUR PHYSICAL BODY

&

THE ABDOMINAL
ENERGY CENTER

When there is birth, there will be death.

When we were children, everything around us seemed huge. When we were adolescents, new sensations felt bigger than we could begin to understand. However much or little we consciously remember of all those physical changes, the one constant is us. Our essence. Our selves. Our singular identities to experience the world and universe through the only bodies we'll ever be given for this journey, which is why our bodies are the most valuable property we'll ever own.

The human body is an amazing "soft machine" as philosopher René Descartes once called it. Our bodies house our minds, thoughts, emotions, unique skills, eternal souls, and our sacred genetic connection to God, the core of who we truly are. Humankind has known this for thousands of years. In fact, ancient yoga texts compare our bodies to priceless chariots, with our senses—sight, smell, hearing, taste, and touch—like five strong horses harnessed to them. Just as the charioteer relies on his horses and they rely on him to take charge and guide them successfully, we rely on our senses and they rely on us to take charge in order to lead successful lives. Christian scriptures use different imagery to express the same truth:

> "Don't you know that you yourselves are God's temple and that God's Spirit dwells in your midst? If anyone destroys God's temple, God will destroy that person; for God's temple is sacred, and you together are that temple."
> —Corinthians 3:16-17

We begin learning about our bodies at birth and continue adjusting to them until death. For example, our final physical development is complete by the age of twenty-five when our brains are fully formed. The full discovery of our spiritual potential occurs by the age of forty. For practically half our lives, we're forming and developing. Therefore, even a completely normal life cycle up to a certain age often leads to us behaving irrationally and abusing our bodies' health.

The fact is we're made up of trillions of cells. The microbial cells outnumber human cells by a ratio of 10:1. They're in all living entities, with their own needs and functions. They're intelligent. They communicate with each other. They know what to do without outside interference. In short, our bodies are communities of trillions of lives.

Every one of our cells has a minus voltage on the inside and a positive voltage on the outside. In other words, every living cell is like a battery, and its energy can be measured in voltages. With the correct diet, meditation, and physical activity, we can store and direct that energy, called *chi* or *prana*, for healing.

New physics shows that we are all energy waves interacting with each other and with every living thing every minute of our lives. Plants, animals, other people, and even the earth itself read and communicate with our vibrations, and we manage our surroundings accordingly. We might see each other as physical entities, but that's an illusion. We're actually interacting waves, which is why one person can affect another just by being in their presence. Quantum physicists who study these waves have confirmed that energy waves are what connect us all, because energy waves can't be separated. Collective waves gathered together are called a field. We're made up of cells, but we're also a field.

Our physical bodies then use their energy centers to produce, contain and exchange pranic energy; and there is a direct connection between the quality of our bodies' physical health and our energy centers. Since the lower center of our Three Suns manifests all information about our bodies' conditions, we can tell a lot about whether our physical health is well or imbalanced. And because we are communities of living entities, our bodies can sense our intentions, our emotions, our love.

We often hear the term "self-love," but just as often, we misunderstand what it means and misinterpret it to imply some kind of egotism. In reality, self-love, and self- compassion, lie at the heart of a meaningful life; one in which we fully embrace the preciousness of our own experience, when our souls pay respect and profound gratitude to the temples we inhabit without judgment, without shame or guilt, without comparing ourselves to others, and celebrate our uniqueness. Just as no two snowflakes are alike, no two people are alike. There is no one else on this earth exactly like you, and it is in this uniqueness where your power lies. Truly knowing and experiencing that fact every minute of your life is the key to witnessing the miraculous complexity of human nature.

Until we have love for ourselves and are fully accepting of our own uniqueness, we can't genuinely give lasting love to anyone else. But once that self-love is strongly embedded in our hearts, it becomes like a rose as it opens its petals layer by layer, spreading its fragrance of love and fulfillment to everyone around us. In truth, love is in our hearts from the moment we're born. We just stop feeling it. We have to remember how it feels to be loved unconditionally, and to love our own existence unconditionally.

We've also lost touch with our bodies, often neglecting them in our dissatisfaction. It's important to reconnect and fall in love with them again. Let your love for your body become a lifelong song of appreciation. Your life is only possible because of it.

There's an easy exercise I've learned and passed along to so many people who have hated their bodies. Thanks to this simple practice, they instead have come to establish deep, loving relationships with their bodies. Find a big mirror, stop for a moment and smile at your reflection in the same way you'd smile at an innocent child asking for your help. Your smile will convey the same warmth in your heart that you'll feel from an urge to help that child, and it will convey the same innate kindness you'll learn to feel toward yourself, which is the basis for all the lessons in this book—they all start with self-love and self-kindness.

And because of all the love, kindness, knowledge, hard-earned experience, untapped potential, and sacred genetic wisdom we carry while we're here, our bodies deserve the finest care we can possibly give them.

While you read these next few paragraphs, please place your hands in the center of your chest just below your sternum, and feel the rise and fall of the breath of life. This will help you establish contact with your body. Softly inhale and exhale... inhale... exhale...

Now, focus on where you've placed your hands and notice that it's the exact spot where they naturally, reflexively go when you're feeling anxious, afraid, or stressed. You might describe that sensation as feeling like butterflies are in your stomach, or like a knot is in your stomach, but you can relieve it by closing your eyes and taking a few deep breaths.

There's a reason why this spot is where your hands instinctively go when sudden emotional upset hits. It's a reason that involves your energy body much more than it involves your physical one. Just below the sternum where your hands have been resting in this exercise, and where they go during your times of emotional disruption, lies your solar plexus energy center. The energy from the solar plexus is connected to the pancreas, stomach, liver, and spleen, and any imbalances in this energy center often manifest in eating disorders or chronic digestive problems.

It's also the home our sense of who we are, and who we're not. It's where our egos and our reflexive aversion to pain and our hedonism live, and when it's out of balance, where our insecurities, fears and negativity live.

The solar plexus energy center also happens to feed our adrenal glands, which secrete adrenaline, the stress hormone and source of the "butterflies" and "knots" in our stomachs. All of which is instinctively known and re-acted to by our autonomic nervous system, the system that performs countless involuntary body functions without our having to think about them, and the system that orders our hands to race to our solar plexus energy center to protect it when it senses potential harm.

This makes it clear how important it is to understand that the best way to keep your solar plexus center balanced and happy. The best way I have found is through good, healthy, well-informed nutritional and exercise habits.

Chapter One

Life in Our Bodies
Cells & Microorganisms

"Tell me what you eat and I will tell you what you are."
— Jean Anthelme Brillat-Savarin

The baby boomer generation is breaking records for being the unhealthiest one in history, and millennials are predicted to have even more health issues. One in five millennials has a mental disorder. There's been a 37 percent increase in teen depression and a 200 percent increase in suicides for ten- to fourteen-year-olds in the last fifteen years. Millennial's physical health is on a similar decline. One study found that American teens averaged the same activity level as sixty-year-olds, and since 1970, obesity has tripled in youth ages six to nineteen.

It's ironic that our ancestors, who led simple primitive lives thousands of years ago, instinctively knew more about healthy eating than we do with all our "sophistication," exhaustive biochemical and nutritional research, and technological "progress." If we're so much more advanced than they were, why are we so universally unhealthy and struggling with every food-related crisis from obesity to malnutrition?

The diet of our early ancestors consisted almost exclusively of grains, fruits, vegetables and dark, hand-ground, whole-grain bread. There were no processed foods, and eating meat was strictly reserved for religious occasions. Women sat in circles preparing communal meals for their families, sharing resources, connecting with each other, all with a quiet reverence for the natural world that provided their sustenance. They didn't live to eat, they ate to live, and they were grateful.

It is often thought that the average lifespan of our ancestors was much shorter than it is today. However, at least by the time of the ancient Greeks, there were a few lucky individuals who lived to a ripe old age, and it is still debated whether the maximum human lifespan has risen significantly. Malnourishment is a likely contributor to early loss of life in many early societies, but the changes that have been made to feed mass populations in the last century have led to widespread adoption of calorie-rich but nutrient-poor diets that are not optimized for healthy aging. In short, you're probably not starving, but your diet also may not be very healthy.

We've all heard the aphorism "you are what you eat." Yet it doesn't really sink in for most of us until some critical moment in our lives when it becomes impossible to ignore.

For example, when I finally understood that my body is ultimately my responsibility, and that this body I've been given is the only one I'll ever have, I started being vigilant about how I treat mine and what I put into it. Before long, I saw a tremendous improvement in how rejuvenated and energized I felt, and how much more available I was to enjoy the whole experience of my life. I've had my share of health issues. I had asthma when I was growing up, as well as stomach problems. I couldn't leave the house in the morning without taking my daily regimen of pills. I also had allergies to a number of things including my beloved pets. (I now have a dog and a cat, by the way, and don't take a single pill—I'm not allergic to them at all.)

Then, by the time I was twenty-one and pregnant with my first child, I'd developed heart issues. And probably buying into the traditional, ridiculous myth that "you're eating for two now," I also gained an unhealthy amount of weight.

I tried a couple of popular weight loss diets and quickly discovered they weren't for me. I wasn't looking for something to just go "on" and then get "off" when my excess weight was gone. I was looking for healthy, long-term answers about nutritious foods. I wanted to know how and why they work. I wanted to understand the digestive system and what I should and shouldn't put into my body. It was time for me to stop guessing about the best fuel I could give myself, and time to take charge and educate myself.

It turned out I had a lot to learn, and a lot to unlearn. Now two decades later, I'm still reaping the benefits from learning and unlearning every single day. I switched to a plant-based diet and that alone has changed my life for the better. My energy level has increased and become steady and reliable, without an unpredictable rollercoaster of highs, crashes, and cravings for stimulants like sweets or coffee. It's helped me be emotionally balanced so that I feel lighter and more optimistic. It's sharpened my mind and ability to focus. In general, it's one of the best health decisions I've ever made.

We'll discuss the details of a plant-based diet later in Part One. But first, let's review some basic facts about the human body. Our bodies are made up of about forty trillion cells, and every minute, three hundred million of them perish; but new ones are also created every minute at a rate of approximately ten to fifty trillion new cells every single day. Because of this daily cycle of renewal, our bodies, even our skin, are automatically and constantly changing. We won't have the same bodies and the same skin a month from now that we have today. But by controlling what we ingest and how we nourish our cells, we have power to influence the quality of our miraculous micro-molecular renewal.

It starts with changing our perception of food. We have to start seeing it not so much as a source of pleasure but as a source of *life*. We have to start focusing on quality, not quantity, and on providing our bodies with the nutrition they need. We have to start thinking of food as the foundation on which our bodies are built. Just as a building can't be strong and durable without a solid foundation, neither can we. We have to take an educated and thoughtful look at our day-to-day diets and ask ourselves, *is what I'm eating nourishing my body or compromising it?*

Another life form living in our bodies, and essential to the balance of our digestive systems, is bacteria. You've probably heard a lot about prebiotic and probiotic foods. There's an excellent reason for their popularity. They can profoundly improve your overall well-being. Prebiotic foods basically nourish the good bacteria in your gut, while probiotic foods contain good bacteria that are extremely beneficial for the health of the gut and overall digestive system.

While medicine addresses only the consequences of diseases, we should also focus on supporting our immune system. We must act to improve our daily diet which in turn directly helps our body fortify its protective functions. Since ancient times, people have identified the quality of a body with the quality of the food consumed. They were then and still are absolutely correct. We must understand the importance of providing our body with the right balance of nutrients to support our physical, mental, and emotional well-being.

A healthy digestive system is key to the health of the whole organism. You are familiar with phrases like "Go with your gut" or "What's your gut telling you?" but now research shows these common expressions may have a scientific basis. It turns out we have a "second brain" residing in our gut.

The billons of neurons in the brain are constantly firing off signals that travel down the long vagus nerve sending messages to many of our inner organs, including to our digestive tract. But our gut has its own army of neurons as well, the so-called Enteric Nervous System (ENS) embedded in the lining of the digestive tract. Around 85 percent of these neurons— there are millions of them—are busy sending messages the other way back up to our brain. Although this connection may harken back to the days when humans were hunter-gatherers and had to rely on "gut instincts" for survival, the link today between our gut and our brain is no less significant.

It's the microorganisms colonizing our gut that play a pivotal role here. The so-called gut bacteria or gut flora form part of a delicately balanced digestive tract ecosystem known as the microbiome. There are around 100 trillion microorganisms living in our large intestine alone, of which 300 to 500 are different species of bacteria. The composition of each person's microbiome is as unique as a fingerprint. There are more bacteria cells than human cells in our bodies. You could even say that we are more bacteria or fungi than human. No matter how unbelievable it sounds, our bodies are conglomerations of different forms of life representing some facet of the universe. And as in any universe, there are a host of forces performing various functions, some of which we understand and some we don't.

As well as aiding digestion and supplying essential nutrients, these microscopic living organisms also impact the rhythm and intensity of our ENS. So the trick is to encourage friendly bacteria that promote well-being both in the gut and beyond. Good gut bacteria can help us build a strong protective system for our body by stabilizing and reinforcing our immune system. Good gut bacteria do not like sweet and processed foods. Good gut bacteria prefer vegetables, fruits, grains, and cereals rich in vitamins, minerals, and fiber.

Illness, stress, fears, sugar, poor diet, and antibiotics can negatively impact our microbiome by reducing the number of good bacteria and allowing the bad ones to colonize the lining of our gut. This can lead to a range of chronic diseases including irritated bowel syndrome, obesity, and cancer. An unhappy gut can also affect our overall mood.

A balanced gut-brain connection, therefore, works both ways. As an example, a change in the microbiome triggers changes in our brain chemistry, and that can have an impact on behavior, mood, memory, and learning capacity. An unstable mood, anxiety, and depression are all linked to the production of serotonin, the "feel-good hormone," and we now know that the microorganisms living in our digestive tract are responsible for manufacturing most of the body's serotonin, a key player in our mental well-being.

In conclusion, our bodies contain countless living organisms that rely on us to nourish them properly, just as we rely on them to keep us alive and healthy. We owe it to them, and to ourselves, to eliminate "empty" foods from our lives and develop a relationship with food that our ancestors instinctively embraced. We can also benefit from adding prebiotics and probiotics to our diet. Prebiotics are available in supplement form and/or you can enjoy them in prebiotic-rich foods like apples, bananas, asparagus, Jerusalem artichokes, garlic, onions, and jicama root. Probiotics are available as well in supplement form and can also be found in foods such as yogurt, a fermented tea called kombucha, fresh sour dill pickles, kimchi (a Korean side dish traditionally made with fermented napa cabbage), sauerkraut, and miso.

This easily accessible plan can lead you to being the healthiest and strongest version of yourself.

Chapter Two

Sweet Enemies, Chronic Inflammation & Fasting

From the moment we take a bite of something, the amazing and involuntary process of digestion begins. Once we put food in our mouths and begin to chew it, our teeth and saliva break it down in preparation for being swallowed. Once it's swallowed, it enters the esophagus, which moves it toward a muscular ring called the sphincter and then into the stomach. The stomach's gastric acid and other digestive juices further break down the food before it's released into the small intestine. The small intestine, liver, and pancreas then go to work with their digestive juices and enzymes to separate the fats, carbohydrates, proteins, minerals, and other nutrients for delivery to the large intestine. There they're absorbed into the bloodstream through the intestinal walls and delivered to the trillions of cells throughout the body. Whatever waste products aren't absorbed into the bloodstream move through the digestive tract and into the colon to be eliminated.

It's a brilliantly efficient system, created to process the natural, single-ingredient foods that nourished our ancestors for thousands of years. But then along came "progress," and with progress came more and more components being added to our food, from dyes to concentrates to preservatives to flavor enhancers to a list of ingredients most of us can't even pronounce. All of them unfamiliar and hostile to our bodies, and almost all of them not adding even a trace of nutritional value.

For thousands of years, the quality of our food was fairly consistent. But in the last fifty to sixty years, it has changed dramatically; and it's no coincidence that as the quality of food has diminished, so has the quality of our health with profound increases in a variety of diseases and health conditions.

So many foreign compounds are being introduced into our digestive systems that our bodies have no idea what to do—they can't even recognize them let alone digest them. All those preservatives, chemicals, and taste and smell enhancers are causing our bodies' biggest challenge: inflammation. Chronic inflammation lies at the root of many allergies and other illnesses. It's the body's way of telling us, "Please stop! Don't do it! No more!"

One result is our bodies don't have time to digest, detox, develop. An intermittent fast is exactly the right solution. For thousands of years, humans and animals have instinctively known to fast when sick as a way to redirect their energy toward healing themselves. Today, fasting has become a huge health and fitness trend due to its guarantee to give our bodies time to refresh and reboot their natural processes. Many religions have also embraced fasting among their practices, even since ancient times. In the Muslim religion, for example, the intermittent diet is a central ritual in which food and water consumption is restricted from sunrise to sunset for one lunar month.

There is some evidence that an intermittent diet can also be a powerful weapon, not only against chronic inflammation, but also against Alzheimer's disease, heart disease, type 2 diabetes, and cancer. It can promote longevity, too. I can personally attest to having experienced great results from an intermittent diet.

There are different durations of intermittent fasting. Some people see results in twenty-four, thirty-six or forty-eight hours depending on individual health issues and willpower. The first twelve hours could be challenging. For instance, you might experience headaches, which occur especially when a lot of toxins get released into the bloodstream.

It's difficult to explain the feeling after fasting, but one way to describe it is being light, refreshed, alert, and mentally clear. You can compare fasting with your computer getting successfully rebooted in that your body gets successfully cleansed and rejuvenated.

The style of fasting I've chosen is known as the 16/8 method, and it's amazingly easy to practice and sustain. It involves setting aside eight hours a day for consuming nutritious foods and beverages, and fasting for the remaining sixteen hours. (Drinking water during the fasting hours is definitely allowed.) You can personalize this intermittent diet based on your schedule.

For example, restricting your eating to the hours between noon and 8:00 p.m. means you can sleep through several hours of your fasting, not bother with breakfast, and still enjoy a nutritious lunch and dinner. Or, if you're an early riser, you might choose 8:00 a.m. to 4:00 p.m., allowing you to eat a healthy breakfast, lunch, and a light snack or early dinner. Another recommended alternative to a regimented breakfast, lunch, or dinner is to enjoy small meals and snacks throughout the eight-hour "eating time" as a way to help stabilize blood sugar levels. You can also choose how often you repeat your 16/8 intermittent fasting practice: once a month, once a week, or even every day if you want. Whichever schedule and frequency you choose, your body will thank you for trying something so simple, healthy, and cleansing.

While we're on the subject of inflammation and the many diseases it can cause, there's ongoing confusion about two of the most common words in any conversation about twenty-first-century nutrition: fat and sugar.

It's a myth that fats make us fat. Yes, there are "bad fats" we should avoid. Saturated ones like those in butter, margarine, certain cuts of meat, whole milk, ice cream, and tropical oils have the potential to increase "bad" cholesterol levels; and trans fatty acids, often just called trans fats, found in fried foods, vegetable shortening, processed snack foods, and baked goods like cakes and pastries cannot only raise "bad" cholesterol levels but also increase the risk of inflammation.

But there are also "good fats" that can improve cholesterol levels and reduce the risk of heart disease. Monounsaturated fats found in nuts, avocados, and vegetable oils, and polyunsaturated fats found in foods like salmon, tofu, canola oil, walnuts, and flaxseeds, are very beneficial for overall health. In fact, omega-3 fatty acids, which are a type of polyunsaturated fat, are so heart-healthy that they've been shown to guard against coronary artery disease and to even help lower blood pressure.

None of this can be said about refined white sugar, which has no nutritional value at all and is guaranteed to do more harm than good, most alarmingly by leading to chronic inflammation no matter how hard a sweet tooth might try to convince us otherwise. Yes, our brains have been genetically and physiologically attracted to sweets for thousands of years. They need glucose, a vital source of energy found in carbohydrates, to function efficiently; and our ancestors relied on natural glucose-rich foods like fruits, honey, and molasses in order to survive. But it wasn't until about four hundred years ago that sugarcane, rich in antioxidants, calcium, and other important nutrients, reached mass-consumption status in the Western world in the form of nutritionally worthless refined sugar. Today, it is nothing more than a potentially addictive carbohydrate. However, our brains are still organically drawn to its sweet taste and energy-building glucosamine, and eagerly welcome it even though an excess of refined sugar is harmful to our well-being.

This sugar diminishes our mental sharpness, focus, memory, and self-control. And there are researchers who claim that refined sugar is eight times more addictive than cocaine. In fact, Dr. Nicole Avena of the Icahn School of Medicine at Mount Sinai tells the *Huffington Post* that pizza is by far the most addictive food due to the hidden sugar—the tomato sauce alone in just one slice can contain more sugar than a handful of Oreos.

Refined sugar also affects our moods by impairing our ability to appropriately process our emotions. It activates a reward-response mechanism in the brain that promotes overeating, not unlike the growing tolerance a drug addict experiences in needing more and more of a drug to keep getting high. It can take up to six weeks to kick a sugar addiction, six weeks that can include withdrawals resembling withdrawals from drugs.

The impact of refined sugar on the body is every bit as dramatic as it is on the brain. It harms blood vessels. It causes our bodies to store fat and therefore gain weight. It can lead to elevated blood pressure and increase the risk of diabetes, all without a single nutritional benefit.

This raises an obvious question: In order to save us and our children from this very real threat to our mental and physical well-being, why isn't there a legally mandated limit on the amount of refined sugar commercial food products can contain?

Fortunately, giving up refined sugars doesn't mean that we have to sacrifice sweet foods. As our ancestors proved thousands of years ago, the earth has blessed us with a number of natural, unprocessed, nutritious alternatives. Seek them out and develop a preference for one or two that your body, brain, and emotions will appreciate.

In conclusion, eliminating inflammation from your body will make an amazing difference in your physical, mental, and emotional wellness. In addition to the ingredients I've already mentioned, here are some others to avoid in order to reduce your risk of inflammation and many other health hazards from what may be hiding in seemingly harmless foods:

1. White flour
2. High fructose corn syrup artificial sweeteners
3. Sodium benzoate and potassium benzoate
4. Butylated hydroxyanisole (BHA—a potentially cancer-causing preservative), sodium nitrates and sodium nitrites
5. Artificial colors blue (1 and 2), green (3), red (3) and yellow (6) (all have been linked to thyroid, adrenal, bladder, kidney, and brain cancers)
6. Monosodium glutamate (MSG, a processed "flavor enhancer") and propyl gallate
7. Sodium benzoate and benzoic acid

Chapter Three

The Truth about Calories

It really is amazing how little is understood about nutrition and its interaction with our bodies. The global belief in calorie counting as an effective way to lose weight is a perfect example.

In 1896, Wilbur Atwater, a professor of chemistry and specialist in human nutritional science at Wesleyan University in Connecticut, conducted a series of experiments. One in particular involved a group of male student volunteers. The students ate what Atwater considered to be a typical American diet, and then exercised with weights, stationary bikes, and treadmills. The amount of heat released by the volunteers at various stages of digestion, exercise, sleep, et cetera, as well as their oxygen intake, carbon dioxide output, and amount of energy provided by the typical American diet they ate, were measured by a machine Atwater invented called the respiration calorimeter. Based on the principle that energy can be changed from one form to another but it can't be created or destroyed, he used the calorimeter to quantify the number of units of energy provided by the food versus the number of units used and left over—the leftover ones would be either stored in the body or excreted. He named these energy units "calories," and now more than 120 years later, a "belief" in the importance of calorie counting is considered a "fact."

The implication that all calories are created equal, and that our bodies process them as if they're all equal—an implication the food industry has enthusiastically promoted since 1896—is simply untrue. If it was true, that would mean, for example, that we'd get the same result from 1,200 calories of cake and ice cream as we would from 1,200 calories of fruits, vegetables, and whole grains. This might work if our bodies had the mechanical complexity of a toaster. But our digestive systems are too physiologically, chemically, hormonally, metabolically, and genetically intricate for us to treat them as if all we need to know to maintain them well is how to add and subtract calories.

Despite this logic, by the 1970s, calorie counting as a means for weight and health management had become thought of as "common knowledge," which made it all the more confusing as to why obesity was on the rise throughout the world. By then, consumption of processed foods and sugar was on the rise as well. But rather than making the connection and cutting back on junk food, the public, with encouragement from the government and lobbyists, chose a new dietary Public Enemy Number One: fat. Since calories couldn't be the culprit, it had to be fat.

If you're worried about getting fat, obviously you should avoid eating some fats, especially since fat is the highest caloric compound in all foods. But back in the 1970s, no distinction was made between good fats and bad fats, not even polyunsaturated ones which our bodies need but can't produce on their own. And the anti-fat movement was underway, with governments and the food industry joining in, endorsing low-fat, low-calorie diets, and replacing them with plenty of tasty sugary, starchy ones. Not coincidentally, starting in 1975, obesity rates began rising at an unprecedented rate. But that didn't deter the misguided movement, and by 1990, food labeling became mandatory in the United States with calorie counts featured at the top of the list. Compounding the effects of this misleading information was that the labeling law didn't necessarily require accuracy; in fact it allowed for a 20 percent margin of error in the calorie count alone.

And then there's the way calorie counts are calculated. They're based on how much heat is released when calories are burned off under laboratory conditions, which happens in that case in a matter of seconds. Whereas the same process in the real world takes our bodies anywhere from minutes to several days. This makes it obvious to question the reliability of those laboratory results.

For example, laboratory ovens can heat food, but they can't break it down into macronutrients and calculate their effects on our bodies. They can't quantify a simple carbohydrate in the food, like refined sugar, which will be quickly absorbed, carried by a sudden release of insulin from the blood-stream into the cells to create a risk of excess of sugar, of which only some of that excess can be stored by the liver and the rest gets stored as fat, and ultimately causes a dip in our blood sugar levels that leaves us feeling hungry. Conversely, complex carbohydrates like whole grains, vegetables, and rice also break down into sugar, but more slowly. One result is complex carbohydrates help keep our blood sugar levels more stable and our appetites satisfied for longer periods of time.

There are also the two main simple sugars in our diet: glucose and fructose. Eaten in the same quantities, they tend to contain the same number of calories. But there's a hunger hormone in the body called ghrelin. Its levels go up when we're hungry and down when we've eaten. Fructose, a common ingredient in processed foods and beverages, can lead to higher ghrelin levels—i.e., more hunger—than the natural glucose found in unprocessed vegetables, fruits, rice, potatoes, and other satisfying foods. Just to clarify, "bad" fructose is a common ingredient in added sugars in processed foods and beverages. Natural, unprocessed fruits contain "good" fructose as well as other essential nutrients such as potassium, vitamin C and fiber, so include plenty of them in your diet.

There are many more examples of how our bodies process food that calorie counting doesn't even take into account. For instance, proteins require more energy for metabolizing than do fats and carbohydrates. Also, the most filling macronutrients help reduce the temptation to overeat. Other factors include whether or not the food is cooked and the length of a person's intestines. And, aside from the fact that we all know weight loss diets don't work for any appreciable amount of time, calorie counting can also lead to an obsessive focus on food.

It's time we stop being manipulated by bad advice, advice that has been proven to be inaccurate, oversimplified, and potentially threatening to our health. We've eaten our way into an epidemic of obesity, diabetes, and heart disease, but we can educate ourselves and our children out of it, back to wellness so that rather than living to eat, we can thrive by eating to live.

Chapter Four

The "Food" Industry

Who doesn't appreciate the convenience of cheap ready-to-eat fast foods, snacks, and beverages? The answer: our bodies. However, we also have to recognize the contribution processed food has made to humankind. If it weren't for cooking, smoking, fermenting, and preserving food, there probably wouldn't be many of us around; and those who make it probably would be hungry and even malnourished.

But then along came the Industrial Revolution and a growing understanding that mass-manufacturing and mass-distributing food products could lead (theoretically) to less world hunger and more company profits. Cheap, fatty, sugary foods, especially bakery goods and desserts, began flooding global markets, and brought with the nutritional chaos, another one of its products, heart disease.

By the 1980s, the food industry had come to a whole new level of realization.

If bigger profits could be made on industrially processed foods, even though they offered virtually no nutritional value, then fortunes could be built. They saw a gold mine in ultra-processed, ready-to-eat, durable, addictive snacks, frozen meals, fast food, cereals, beverages, energy bars, et cetera, manufactured not from whole foods but from ingredients *refined* from whole foods like cheap remnants of animal parts, artificial sugars, plenty of starches, and all the hydrogenated fats anyone could dream of—hydrogenation being a chemical process that can turn liquid oils into solids full of trans fats which are notoriously linked to, among other things, coronary artery disease.

Adding in aggressive global advertising and the population's then relatively new habit of eating potato chips, corn chips, pretzels, and the likes in between meals; and increasing availability of ultra-processed foods at supermarkets, fast-food chains and convenience stores, wasn't a formula corporations had to work too hard for. It was as easy as printing money for a global population clamoring for more, even though it suffered at the same from increases in obesity, type-2 diabetes, heart disease, strokes, and abnormal cholesterol levels more than ever before.

It's obscene that corporations make vast fortunes off of their cheap ultra-processed products with full knowledge of the damage they're inflicting on public health. Between hiring lobbyists, filing lawsuits, sowing confusion, and avoiding regulation, they have found ways to hook us into accepting their food-like substances designed to keep us and our children perpetually hungry, perpetually unsatisfied, and perpetually compromised.

Fortunately, the ultra-processed food industry isn't in charge of our physical health. We are. We weren't born with a preference for junk food. Bad eating habits are learned, which means they can be unlearned. We can put a stop to being victimized by manufacturers who don't have our best interests at heart by rejecting their inferior, health-endangering products and returning to an endless variety of whole, natural, nutritious, single-ingredient foods our amazing planet provides. Foods that kept our ancestors strong and healthy for thousands of years before all this dietary "progress" and the diseases it brought came along.

Chapter Five

Vegan
To Be, Or Not To Be

The question of whether humans are naturally herbivores (vegetarians) or naturally carnivores (meat eaters) is a controversy that has been debated among nutritionists for decades; however, evidence shows that we're more physiologically likely to be herbivores. For example, there's the first essential step of ingesting food, the chewing process. Carnivores' jaws, designed to tear flesh and crush food, exclusively move up and down. Whereas human jaws can move both up and down and from side to side, closer to the structure of herbivores. This allows us to grind plant foods with our molars.

Carnivores also have short gastrointestinal tracts. The intestinal tract ratio of herbivores is much longer, including in humans, which means it takes longer for meat to pass through the digestive system. In fact, meat can remain in our intestines for up to three days, increasing the risk of inflammation and chronic diseases.

Then there's the issue of stomach acidity. We normally have a healthy level of stomach acid produced by glands in the stomach lining, that, along with enzymes, break down the food we eat. But carnivores have significantly higher stomach acidity levels, way above what's normal for us, to help digest meat and bones and fight off bacteria that can lead to infection.

A number of studies show that a human diet rich in animal protein increases the production of the growth hormone IGF-1, too much of which may trigger colon, prostate, and breast cancer; increase levels of an organic compound called TMAO (trimethylamine N-oxide) in the bloodstream, which can cause heart disease; and raise levels of high sensitivity C-reactive protein, which is a marker for inflammation. The growth in meat consumption, coupled with the worsening environment and resulting diminished quality of food, might also be a reason for the increase in cases of both colon and several types of stomach cancer.

So, with all these indications that humans might really be natural-born herbivores, and having ancestors who strictly reserved meat-eating for religious holidays and festivals, the question is, why have we become such avid meat eaters?

The answer is primarily linked to industrial progress. Meat production has grown almost five-fold in the past fifty years and become a multi-billion-dollar industry. Intensive and increasingly profitable farming practices have made animal products more readily available, which in turn has driven up the global appetite for meat and the resulting higher level of consumption than ever before.

There is no "one-size-fits-all" plan for healthy eating. Everyone is different, chemically, hormonally, metabolically, genetically, and physiologically, so it's up to you, your doctor, and your nutritionist to decide what works best for you. Being a vegan, I believe that meat should be consumed in moderation. I'm against any fanatical radicalization where vegans make bad jokes about meat lovers and meat lovers retaliate with the same disrespect. I do not encourage a total elimination of meat from everyone's diet because I believe that your body is your business. We all have to build our own personal, loving relationship with our bodies and meet our own healthiest nutritional needs.

My decision to become a vegan was based largely on my intensive studies into how our bodies work, but there was also a definite ethical consideration as well. The meat industry should take a lesson from our ancestors, because the way animals are slaughtered today is simply unacceptable. In the days when eating meat was reserved for special occasions, animals were sacrificed with great respect and with a certainty that they felt no fear. Prayers were recited and offerings given to remove negative energy and karma, and to make the meat more suitable for consumption by eliminating the animal's stress hormones.

There's no question that cows are intelligent, feeling creatures. They experience sadness, anxiety, panic, and a whole range of other emotions. Studies have found that when a member of a human family dies, a cow belonging to that family can mourn, including with tears pouring down its face; and also that cows and their calves can display extreme distress when they're separated. It is clear then that a cow awaiting slaughter understands what's about to happen, feels terror, and releases a high level of stress hormones that may present a health risk to the human who consumes the meat. In fact, it's my belief that in addition to those stress hormones, eating any emotionally developed mammal also means eating their karma, the information stored in the form of energy. Animals and every other living thing on this planet have the same energy field as humans. It's an energy field that connects us all.

As a vegan, I'm frequently asked: "How can someone following a vegetarian or vegan diet get enough protein without eating meat?" Sometimes when I answer I feel like I'm talking to a bunch of professional bodybuilders whose only focus is their physical shape and muscle growth. But usually when I answer them, I sense they are so far from a healthy and nutritious lifestyle that I am hoping they will stop and think when I ask in return: "Where do you get *your* protein? Are you getting enough nutrition from *your* diet?"

The truth is, all foods contain some protein; and of course, everyone following a vegan diet should eat a variety of plant-based foods to get the required range of amino acids. There is also a variety of good plant-based proteins on the market, especially if you need extra building blocks for your muscles to help them recover after strenuous exercise. Meat products provide us with secondary-source protein since the animals that are consumed obtain their protein directly from plants. We can only get primary-source protein and other necessary building blocks for our bodies by "eliminating the middleman" and eating those plants ourselves.

My decision to turn vegan was easy. I was never much of a meat eater to begin with, so giving it up entirely wasn't a challenge. But "vegan" meant eliminating all animal products from my diet, including dairy. I lived in Switzerland for many years, where dairy products were among my staples. I thought I would never be able to eliminate them from my diet, especially yogurt and cheese, but I made a commitment to myself and was determined to keep it.

I was surprised at how hard it was for me to give up cheese, although I did appreciate that for some reason the migraine headaches I had been suffering from completely disappeared. I found the answers to that mystery later when I read about a study conducted by scientists at the University of Michigan. They discovered that cheese contains a chemical also found in addictive drugs. That chemical, casein, is found in all dairy products. When casein breaks down in the stomach, it produces a peptide called casomorphin, an opioid, and it triggers the opioid receptors in the brain. Casein also acts as a histamine releaser, which explains why many people are allergic to dairy products.

The more I explored the subject of dairy products, the happier I was with my decision to never eat them again. There's an ongoing discussion about dairy products' effect on our health, but it's inarguable that dairy from large industrial enterprises don't offer the same quality and health benefits as those produced on small farms. It's also a fact that many of us, and our children, are lactose intolerant without knowing it, which causes many health problems that can be hard to trace the roots of and diagnose.

I also came across the writings of biochemist Dr. Colin Campbell, professor emeritus of nutritional biochemistry at Cornell University, who has devoted himself to extensive studies in nutrition, biochemistry, and microbiology, with a primary focus on the connection between diet and disease. Campbell has written prolifically on his belief that "common knowledge" about nutrition, which starts in elementary school, isn't designed by science, but instead is manufactured by the massive influence of the food manufacturing industry. Among his many discoveries and theories during his twenty-seven-year-long study called The China Project, is that because of the casein found in all animal protein, cow's milk doesn't seem to be intended for human consumption. Not only does the casein in cow's milk create a condition called metabolic acidosis, for which the body compensates by draining calcium from our bones—which is ironic considering that many of us were raised on the belief that "milk builds strong bones"—it also turns out to be "the most relevant chemical carcinogen ever identified" as both an activator and accelerator of cancer. Campbell is one of many nutritional experts who are gratified to see that many countries, including Canada, are restructuring their nutritional guidelines to promote a whole-foods, plant-based diet.

I imagine some of you are thinking that a plant-based diet means a lifetime of nothing but grazing in pastures like herds of livestock. But after many years of veganism, I can assure you that if you decide it's worth trying, you will have a wide variety of delicious, satisfying foods to look forward to.

Plus, a vitality and enthusiasm that you might have thought you'd lost.

The wonders of the botanical world are more than enough to sustain us and help us evolve. The seasons of the year speak to us, if we listen. Nature has a biological tempo that is connected to all. In winter, for instance, oats, cereals, and grains can become staples that warm, comfort, and restore us. Even each day has its own pattern and poetry, from dawn to dawn. What does all of this mean for our bellies? It means that each moment, each meal, has its own rhythm and ritual as well. Ancient grains, as an example, are brimming with micro-elements and are fantastic staples for vegans. Combination bowls with these grains have become popular superfoods packed with proteins, fresh greens, and juicy flavors.

Everyone needs to eat, but how can we elevate this fuel beyond survival? How can our eating habits guide us to thrive, to live our most harmonious lives? How can we experience harmony with food? Let's honor our materiality and celebrate our bodies. Let's nourish our minds and souls. Let's find as much balance as we can so we can be present and at peace more and more.

If your current diet is providing you with the maximum physical, mental, and emotional health you deserve, I applaud you and encourage you to stay with it. But if you're curious to find out if veganism can make life-changing differences in your body, mind, and emotions the way it has in mine, experiment with it for a few days or a week.

To help encourage you to give a plant-based, high-frequency diet a try, I'm happy to share a three-day regimen that includes breakfast, lunch, dinner, and snacks, along with the recipes, to foster your resilience and reverie. They're delicious, satisfying, and guaranteed to maximize your health and strengthen your immune system. Bon appétit!

Morning Ritual

Chia seed chocolate pudding
Açai bowl ice cream
Blueberry oatmeal bread

Noon Ritual

Magical Mushroom Medley with quinoa
Asparagus spaghetti, tahini and toasted pistachios

Afternoon Ritual

Sweet potato brownie bites
Avocado toast and zucchini fritters
Buffalo cauliflower wings
Rainbow toast

Evening Ritual

Brilliant Thai yellow peanut curry
Mung beans with fresh veggies
Mushroom risotto
Midwinter night's ratatouille
Caramelized maple broccoli

Morning Ritual

Galaxy Chia Pudding Stars

3-8 oz. Resealable glass jars
7 tbsp. Black chia seeds
16 oz. Fresh coconut milk
2 tbsp. Unsweetened cacao powder
2 tbsp. Maple syrup

1. Place 2 tbsp of chia seeds in each of the 3 jars.
2. Place liquid ingredients and cocoa powder into a blender and pulse until combined.
3. Pour unequal amounts over chia seeds into each jar.
4. Stir to combine.
5. Cover and refrigerate overnight. E voila!

Morning Ritual

Moonlight Almond Açai Bowl

2 frozen bananas
1 frozen acai pack
1 Lemon, juiced
1c. Almond milk
2 tbsp. grade B maple syrup

1. Place all ingredients into a blender and puree until smooth and creamy. Serve over granola. Namaste!

Morning Ritual

Dawn's Early Light Oatmeal Loaf

1 c. Coconut milk
½ c. Grade B maple syrup
1 banana
1 tsp. Vanilla
1 c. Oat flour
1 c. Quick cook rolled oats
⅓ c. Tapioca flour
1 tsp. Baking soda
1 tsp. Cinnamon
½ tsp. Salt
¼ tsp. Nutmeg
2 cups fresh blueberries
1 c. Granola

1. Preheat oven to 360°F.
2. Grease a glass baking dish.
3. Combine coconut milk, maple syrup, banana and vanilla in a blender, blend until combined and set aside.
4. Combine all dried ingredients except granola.
5. Place blueberries in the bottom of the baking dish, top with batter.
6. Sprinkle granola on top of batter. Bake for 25-30 minutes until golden and cooked through.
   Enjoy!

Noon Ritual

Magic Mushroom Medley

1 c. Quinoa

2 c. Water or vegetable stock

2 cups quartered mushrooms

1 tbsp. Vegetable oil

½ White onion, quartered and thinly sliced

½ Red pepper, quartered and thinly sliced

1 lb. Asparagus, trimmed and cut into 2" pieces

1 tbsp. Soy sauce

4 c. Fresh spinach leaves

2 tbsp. Pepitas salt to taste

1. Heat a small sauce pan to medium high.
2. Add and toast quinoa for 3-4 minutes.
3. Add water or stock, ¼ tsp. Salt, and stir. Bring to a boil, cover, and cook for 15 minutes. Fluff with a fork and set aside.
4. Heat a dry pan to medium heat.
5. Add mushrooms and cook for 15 minutes until most of the moisture has evaporated and the flavors are concentrated.
6. Season with salt and set aside.
7. In another pan, heat oil over medium heat, add onions and cook for 2-3 minutes. Add peppers and continue to cook over medium heat until onions are translucent. Season with salt and set aside.
8. In another pan, heat oil over medium heat, add asparagus and cook for 3-5 minutes, add soy sauce and toss.
9. Combine mushrooms, onion and pepper mixture, asparagus and cooked quinoa. Mix it with the fresh green spinach leaves.
10. Top with pepitas and season with salt. Delish!

Noon Ritual

Springtime Asparagus

1 c. Quinoa
2 c. Water or vegetable stock
1 c. Cooked garbanzo beans
1 c. Asparagus ribbons
1 tbs. Lemon zest
¼ c. Chiffonade of basil
¼c. Chopped pistachios

+ Dressing:
1 c. Mint leaves
½ c. Water
½c. Tahini
¼ c. Lime juice
1 tbsp. Maple syrup salt
to taste

1. Heat a small sauce pan over medium high heat.
2. Add quinoa and toast for 3-4 minutes.
3. Add water or stock, ¼ tsp. Salt and stir.
4. Bring to a boil, cover and cook for 15 minutes. Fluff with a fork and set aside.
5. To make dressing, put tahini, lime juice, maple syrup, mint leaves into a blender and blend until smooth. Check for seasoning.
6. Use vegetable peeler to slice the stalks of fresh asparagus lengthwise into very thin strips.
7. Toss quinoa and thin ribbons of raw asparagus together. Add half of the dressing to coat.
8. Add more if needed.
9. Top with pistachios
10. Season with salt.
    Pass around!

Afternoon Ritual

Brownie Bites

7 oz. Dates, chopped
2 small sweet potatoes, peeled, cubed and boiled until tender
8 oz. cashews soaked at room temp for about 2 hours
1 avocado
1 tsp. Vanilla
2 tbsp. Maple syrup
½ c. Coconut milk
¼ c. Cacao powder
5 oz. Stone ground flour
1 tsp. Baking powder
¼ tbsp. Salt

1. Combine dates, sweet potatoes, cashews, avocado, vanilla and maple syrup into blender, and puree until smooth.
2. Add coconut milk with blender running.
3. Combine all dry ingredients into a large bowl.
4. Add wet ingredients and fold.
5. Fold onto prepared baking sheet and bake.
6. Bake at 375°F for 25-30 min

Taste the golden glow!

Afternoon Ritual

Zucchini Fritters

3 c. Grated zucchini, salt, then squeeze excess liquid
1 c. Fresh corn kernels
1 c. Cooked quinoa
3 Green onions, finely chopped
⅓ c. Flour
1 tbsp. Baking powder
1 tsp. Garlic powder
1 tsp. Salt

1. Combine all ingredients, form into patties, roll in flour.
2. Cook over medium high heat until golden and cooked through.

Feast!

Afternoon Ritual

Hot Wings!

1 medium size cauliflower, broken into small florets
Spray oil
¼ c. Flour
1 tsp salt
½ c. Plant based milk
Almond, oat, hemp
½ c. Bread crumbs 1 tsp.
Garlic powder
1 tsp. Paprika
1 tsp. Onion powder
½ tsp. Black pepper
½ tsp. Cumin
¼ c. Hot sauce
¼ c. Vegan butter, melted

1. Preheat oven to 425°F.
2. Prepare a sheet pan with parchment and spray with oil.
3. Place cauliflower florets, spray with oil and toss to coat.
4. Place flour and salt into a ziplock bag, add cauliflower and toss to coat.
5. Add milk and toss to coat.
6. In a separate bowl combine bread crumbs, garlic, paprika, onion powder, cumin and black pepper.
7. Add cauliflower and coat evenly with bread crumb mixture.
8. Spread out evenly onto a sheet pan and cook for 25 minutes.
9. Mix hot sauce and butter in bowl.
10. Toss cauliflower with sauce mixture and return to sheet pan. Cook for an additional 10 minutes.
Serve with love!

Afternoon Ritual

Rainbow Toast

½ package soft or medium soft tofu, cut into thin slices
2 tbsp. Rice wine vinegar
2 tbsp. Sweet black vinegar or sweet plum vinegar
¼ c. Soy
¼ c. Grade B maple syrup
½ tsp. Garlic powder
1 green onion, thinly sliced
2 Avocados, mashed
¼ White onion, thinly sliced
½ Small tomato chopped
¼ tsp. Salt
4 slices of toast

1. Place tofu in a single layer to fit tightly in a sealable container. Whisk vinegars, soy and maple garlic powder in a bowl.
2. Pour over tofu and top with green onions.
3. Marinate overnight in refrigerator.
4. Mash avocado, add onion, tomato and salt.
5. Spread toast thickly with avocado and top with marinated tofu slices.

Taste the rainbow!

Evening Ritual

Sunset Curry with a Kick

1 cup brown rice
1 ½ c. Water
½ tsp. Salt
2 tbsp. Vegetable oil (can be safflower, coconut or vegetable)
1 White onion, quartered and thinly sliced
½ Large carrot, peeled, halved lengthwise and thinly sliced into half moons
1 ½ inch knob of fresh ginger, peeled and thinly sliced
2 cloves of garlic, minced
1 14oz. Can organic coconut milk
1 14oz. Whole peeled tomatoes, hand crushed
1 ½ c. Water
1 tbsp. Corn starch
¼ c. Yellow curry
2 tbsp. Soy sauce
2 tbsp. Creamy peanut butter
2 tbsp. Brown sugar, date syrup or agave
1 small sweet potato, peeled, cut into 1" cubes
½ small cauliflower, cut into florets,
½ c. Garbanzo beans
1 c. Quartered mushrooms
1 c. Extra firm tofu, cut into 1" cubes
2 tbps. Lime juice
2 tbsp. Chopped cilantro
salt to taste

1. Bring rice, water and salt (¼ teaspoon per cup of rice) to a boil.
2. Cover and reduce to a slow, steady simmer.
3. Cook for 40 minutes and remove from heat. A wide, shallow pot with a tight-fitting lid ensures evenly cooked grains.
4. Let the cooked rice sit covered for 10 minutes to absorb maximum moisture, then remove the lid and fluff the grains with a fork. Put it aside.
5. Heat oil in a pan over medium heat, add onions and cook for 2-3 minutes.
6. Add carrots, season with salt and cook until onions are translucent.
7. Add ginger, then garlic. Cook for 2 minutes.
8. Add coconut milk, tomatoes, water, corn starch, yellow curry, soy sauce, peanut butter and brown sugar. Cook until blended.
9. Add sweet potatoes and cauliflower, cook until soft and sauce is thickened for 15-20 minutes.
10. Add mushrooms, garbanzo beans and tofu.
11. Cook 5-7 minutes.
12. Add lime juice and cilantro, adjust seasoning with salt. Serve with the brown rice.

Take a spoonful for yourself!

Evening Ritual

Mung Bean Popcorn Bites

1 tbsp. Vegetable oil
½ White onion, quartered and thinly sliced
½ Carrot, quartered and thinly sliced
1 Clove garlic, minced
1 c. Dried mung beans
2 c. Water
¼ c. Crushed tomato
½ tsp. Garlic powder
½ tsp. Paprika
½ tsp. Cumin
1 tsp. Salt
¼ tsp. Black pepper

1. Soak overnight in room temperature water in proportion of 1:2 mung beans.
2. Heat oil in sauce pan over medium high heat. Add onions and cook 3-4 minutes.
3. Add carrots and cook until onions are translucent. Add garlic and cook for 1 minute more.
4. Add mung beans, stir to combine.
5. Add water and bring to a boil.
6. Cover and let simmer for 40 minutes.
7. Add tomato, garlic powder, paprika, cumin, salt and pepper. Store to combine and recover.
8. Cook for 10 more minutes or until beans are tender and liquid is absorbed. Check seasoning before serving.
Munch on as many as you like!

Evening Ritual

Mermaid Pearl Risotto

6 oz. Mushrooms, quartered
2 tbsp. Oil
½ Yellow onion, quartered and thinly sliced
1 c. Pearled barley
2 1/2-3 c. Water or vegetable stock
2 tbsp. Vegan butter
1 tsp Salt

1. Soak overnight in room temperature water in proportion of 1:2 pearled barley.
2. Put mushrooms in hot dry pan and cook 20 minutes until concentrated and browned.
3. Heat oil in pan, cook onions until translucent for 5 minutes. Add to mushrooms and set aside.
4. Add pearled barley and liquid to sauce pan, season with salt.
5. Bring to a boil, cover, reduce to a simmer and cook for 40 minutes. Add butter, onions and mushrooms to combine.
6. Cover and cook for additional 10 minutes.
7. Check for seasoning.
   Celebrate!

Evening Ritual

Hearty, Heartful Ratatouille

¼ c. Olive oil
1 Eggplant, cut into large 1 ½" chunks
2 Zucchini, cut into large 1 ½" chunks
1 Large yellow squash, cut into large 1 ½" chunks
1 Red pepper, cut into large 1 ½" chunks
1 Yellow pepper, cut into large 1 ½" chunks
½ Yellow onion
1 Small tomato, halved
1 tbsp. Salt
1 tsp dry oregano
½ c. Fresh basil, chopped
1 c. Crushed tomatoes
¼ yellow onion, thinly sliced
1 tbsp. Lemon zest

1. Preheat oven to 425°F.
2. Drizzle half of olive oil onto large baking sheet.
3. Spread out separately on pan the eggplant, zucchini, peppers and squash. Place onion and tomato halves in corner of pan.
4. Drizzle remaining olive oil on top of vegetables, season with salt and toss.
5. Roast eggplant for 25 minutes, then remove.
6. Roast peppers for an additional 10 minutes, then remove.
7. Roast zucchini and yellow squash an additional 10 minutes, then remove.
8. Place tomato puree in sauce pan and reduce over medium low heat until thickened. Toss all ingredients together and check for seasoning. Savor every bite!

Evening Ritual

Caramelized Broccoli

1 bunch broccoli, stems
peeled and each head cut
into quarters, lengthwise
3 Cloves of garlic, smashed
2 tbsp. Sweet plum vinegar
2 tbsp. Maple syrup
2 tbsp. Soy sauce
2 tbsp. Lemon juice
2 tbsp. Vegetable oil
1 tbsp. Lemon zest

1. Add 1 tbsp. Oil to wide pan, heat to medium high.

2. Add broccoli in one layer and cook for 5-7 minutes on each side until slightly browned. Halfway through, add the garlic to pan and brown.

3. Mix remaining ingredients in small bowl.

4. Add mixture to pan, reduce heat and toss broccoli until glazed for 2-3 minutes. Hug your family!

Chapter Six

A Balanced Daily Diet & High-Frequency Foods

"Let food be thy medicine and medicine be thy food."
— Hippocrates

Taking in the volumes of information on healthy diets and on new ways to nourish ourselves can be confusing. You can be an expert on nutritional values and try different meal plans occasionally, but still face each day asking, "What am I supposed to eat?"

I see weight loss diets in general as ineffective. Most of them you start and then quit, which only creates more frustration for yourself. Instead, it's important to create a lifestyle that builds a solid base for a healthy body. Those lifestyle habits have to consist of a commitment to what you will eat and what you won't eat.

Our brains may get confused about food, but our bodies won't. They reward us when they're nourished properly. When you adopt eating habits in which fresh, healthy, high-frequency foods are a priority, your body will perform at its peak potential and send you positive feedback without requiring your strong discipline. When you start seeing the first results from a lifestyle of healthy eating and feel the positive changes in your body, there's nothing tempting about being offered something unhealthy. You won't want it, and will simply say, "No, thank you."

Many people, after experiencing a serious health issue, switch to a nutritious regimen and end up changing their eating habits for the rest of their lives. Usually, major health problems caused by stress, or by wrong foods, or by alcohol or tobacco consumption, appear at around age thirty-five to forty-five. That's typically when the clock starts to show us the causation between our choices and our outcomes. It's a far better idea to avoid health crises in the first place by learning how to treat ourselves well, rather than giving those crises a chance to wreck our lives.

Those of us who have pets are careful to make sure that the food we buy for them is perfectly balanced with all the necessary building blocks for their bodies. We are their caretakers. We know perfectly well how to feed them, and we also know perfectly well how not to feed them so that we don't shorten their lives. We pay attention to commercials about their food, how its carefully selected ingredients and amazing quality makes our pets' coats shiny and their teeth strong, puts them in a cheerful, playful mood, and increases their physical activity.

I wonder why we don't sponsor those same kinds of informative advertisements for *our* food. Why, in all those enticing ads about tasty fast foods, is it never mentioned that they're unhealthy, and even harmful? Why do most of us have no idea about which food is good for us and which is not? Which can lead to health and which to disease? Why are so many of us more diligent about staying informed on the right nutritional balance for our pets than we are for ourselves?

In the end, it's our individual responsibility to decide what we put into our bodies and what we don't. It's our choice to either nurture or neglect our bodies. It hardly seems a choice since nurturing them is a gift to ourselves that will keep on giving throughout our lives.

That's why understanding the vibrational frequency of foods is such an essential element in choosing a nutritional plan. It's imperative that we select high-frequency foods that correlate with the frequency of our bodies. Our health depends on the invisible energy we receive from food. There are high-frequency foods—fruits, vegetables, berries, etc.—that contain more prana, energy, and light absorbed from their surroundings and from the sun. And there are low-frequency ones—processed meals, red meat, alcohol, etc.—thought of as dead foods devoid of prana, energy, and light.

It is well known that the human body generates mechanical vibrations. Those vibrations are produced by cells, microorganisms, heartbeats, the respiratory and vascular systems, and other processes. Different organs of the body produce different resonant frequencies.

The brilliant inventor, engineer, and futurist Nikola Tesla once wrote, "If you could eliminate certain outside frequencies that interfered with our bodies, we would have greater resistance toward disease." Lower frequencies lead to a number of health problems. For example, they weaken the immune system and cause blockages in our bodies because our energy can't move freely, which then creates stagnation in our blood circulation. Whereas consuming "life," or high-frequency foods, can raise our body frequency and enhance our overall health. In fact, a vegan diet correlates perfectly with a high-frequency body.

Some fascinating new studies have been done in this field of body frequencies and food frequencies. For instance, Dr. Valerie Hunt, professor emeritus in the UCLA Department of Physiological Sciences, developed a means for mapping human bioenergy fields. She discovered that each of us has a unique resting pattern, which she called the Signature Field.

In an interview with Susan Barber titled "The Promise of Bioenergy Fields: An End to All Disease" for *The Spirit of Ma'at* magazine, Hunt explains that "the Signature Field of a healthy human being is composed of balanced, coherent energy patterns across the full spectrum of frequencies." She goes on to say, "The Signature Field of human beings who have [or are soon going to develop] disease are of two kinds: deficiency patterns and hyperactive patterns... Deficiency diseases like cancer and fatigue syndrome... and hyperactive conditions like colitis, hypertension, and skin problems show anticoherent patterns."

In 1992, a plant geneticist named Bruce Tainio of Tainio Technology, an independent division of Eastern State University in Cheny, Washington, built a calibrated frequency monitor. His findings on the frequencies of both the human body and various foods strongly support beliefs that when the body's frequency drops, the immune system is compromised; that every disease has a frequency; and that ingesting higher-frequency foods can destroy lower-frequency diseases. Other studies show maintaining a 62–72 MHz body frequency is healthiest.

All of this confirms Nikola Tesla's observation about the correlation between outside frequencies and our resistance to disease. Or, to paraphrase another Tesla quote, if you want to understand your body, think in terms of energy, frequency, and vibration.

Thus, in order to maximize the nutritional value of our diets, it's important that we choose foods that contain high-vibration energy. This will help us raise our own auric frequency and connect us with our higher Source. At even the smallest level, our cellular energy can also be significantly increased by committing to high-vibration foods. High-vibrational regimens consist of foods that are nutritionally alive due to their ability to photosynthesize sunlight into energy. In contrast, lower megahertz vibrations from consuming animal products and processed foods decrease our cellular energy and body frequency.

Some religions even practice fasts that exclude all animal products in order to raise their followers' vibrations. And from a purely biological point of view, regularly eating low-vibration foods over time can reduce the body's pH balance and make it vulnerable to bad bacteria, viruses, and funguses. There is a theory based on lab results that suggests cancer cells thrive in an acidic low-pH environment but cannot survive in alkaline high-pH surroundings. What this suggests is that not only is it critical for our well-being to retain a constant pH balance in our blood, but also that alkaline diets containing high-frequency foods with an emphasis on fruits and veggies are the healthiest.

Here are the top fifteen alkaline foods you can add to your diet to maintain a healthy pH balance: cucumbers, seeded watermelon, avocado, spinach, kale, broccoli, lemons, asparagus, papaya, almonds, wheatgrass, bananas, celery, cayenne peppers, and bell peppers.

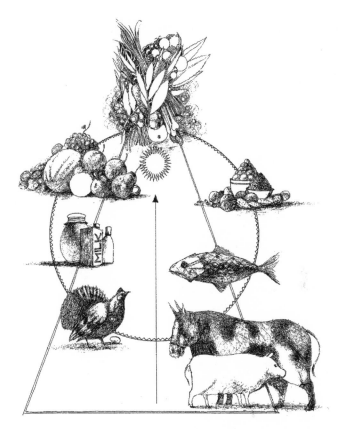

Further clinical research shows that therapeutic grade essential oils have the highest frequency of any natural substance. Essential oils are powerful tools for maintaining and raising vibrational fields. This information is worth a separate book all its own, and I suggest you do more research before you begin using any essential oils.

Food is receptive to our vibrations as well. From my personal experience, it's important to maintain a positive attitude while cooking and serving meals for yourself and your family. Take time to give blessings and gratitude for the food that's about to nourish you and those who worked hard to make it available to you. You will sense how this practice improves the quality of the meal's energy vibration, which in turn will improve yours as well.

Proportion is another important consideration when selecting and maintaining a healthy diet. An easy way to remember the ideal daily balance is to visualize a plate filled with the following approximate proportions:

30 percent greens: broccoli, spinach, lettuce, and other vegetables

30 percent protein: eggs, fish or other seafood, skinless chicken breast; for vegetarians and vegans: oats, quinoa, lentils, soybeans, seeds (chia, pumpkin, sunflower, hemp, etc.), spelt, teff, tofu, tempeh, spirulina, edamame, chickpeas, green peas, most varieties of beans, and Ezekiel bread and other breads made from sprouted grains ·

30 percent carbs: sweet potatoes, pumpkin, corn, oatmeal, pearl barley, brown rice, fruits, and berries

10 percent healthy fats: avocado, almonds and cashews, seeds (chia, pumpkin, sunflower, etc.), and various plant oils, particularly coconut, avocado, and olive

A balanced daily diet doesn't mean a lack of variety nor deprivation. Plus, many of these desirable foods offer hidden benefits. For instance, chia seeds, a superfood that has been known of for thousands of years and is now making a worldwide comeback, are not only great sources of protein and healthy fats, they're also rich in the heart-healthy omega-3 fatty acids that play an important role in regulating a healthy metabolism. (Chia means "strength" in Mayan. It was prized by the Aztecs as a superfood as far back as 3500 BCE.) Other omega-3-rich foods include spinach, papaya, brussels sprouts, pumpkin seeds, soybeans, pecans, eggs, and seafood. Seeds in general are very potent, so you don't have to eat a lot of them to get benefits. One and a half tablespoons per meal is enough.

Spirulina is another one of my favorite superfoods. It is a type of blue-green algae that can be taken as a dietary supplement. It is considered to be a superfood due to its excellent nutritional value and health benefits. Spirulina is 60 percent protein, which is double the amount of protein in red meat, and it is also a great source of phytonutrients, copper, iron, manganese, potassium, B vitamins, iodine, and Gamma-linolenic acid (GLA). It is a powerful antioxidant with anti-inflammatory properties too, in large part due to it containing essential 18 amino acids. There is an opinion that spirulina could also potentially end world hunger. According to economist Urs Heierli, PhD, a sustainable approach to combatting malnutrition is available by giving just one gram of spirulina a day to small children. This idea is supported by the United Nation.

Many people also thrive on macrobiotic diets. I've incorporated many of those principles into my veganism. The macrobiotic diet is based on the Asian philosophy of yin and yang energies and is aimed at achieving balance between our bodies' organs. Its key elements are whole grains, beans, and vegetables, which are thought by some researchers to lower the risk of heart disease and diabetes, lower cholesterol levels and blood pressure, and improve the health and efficiency of the digestive system.

Whole grains are prebiotics, a type of fiber that feeds the probiotics, or good bacteria, in the large intestine. Consuming prebiotics keeps the probiotics functioning efficiently, which leads to overall better gut health. Research also indicates that eating whole grain foods such as cereals, brown rice, and barley increases the number of the good bacteria named bifidobacteria and lactobacilli. The result is a boost to the immune system, diminished gut inflammation, and increased production of butyrate, an essential metabolite in the colon.

For a macrobiotic diet, organically grown whole grains like brown rice, oats, and corn should comprise around 60 percent of the daily diet; locally grown organic vegetables should comprise around 30 percent; and 10 percent should be devoted to beans, bean products, sea vegetables, fermented soy products, seeds, nuts, and fruit. Meats, dairy, processed foods, tropical fruits, fruit juices, poultry, and vegetables like eggplant, tomatoes, and asparagus are advised against. While a traditional macrobiotic diet includes fish, it's easy for vegetarians and vegans to modify it by simply excluding seafood and adding supplements like iron, zinc, and omega-3 fatty acids.

In summary, the higher the frequency of foods we eat to maintain a healthy 62–72 MHz body frequency, the healthier our bodies will be and the more armed we'll be against low-frequency diseases. Fresh foods and fresh herbs are particularly beneficial, while the processed and canned foods making up a majority of most diets are of zero benefit. Whichever regimen you choose, you owe it to yourself and to the long-term health of your body to make a balanced, high-frequency daily diet a way of life.

Chapter Seven

The Gluten-Free Diet Myth

Gluten intolerance can be a very real and incurable condition. In many cases, it has also unfortunately become a popular, often self-diagnosed non-existent condition by people who don't even know the answer to, "What is gluten?"

When I was living in Europe and enjoying French baguettes and pizza, I never thought about gluten. But when I moved to Los Angeles, I was immediately inundated with warnings about the gluten allergy. Later, I realized it's another fashionable cause.

About one percent of the US population suffers from celiac disease. It is a genetic autoimmune disorder in which the ingestion of gluten triggers the production of antibodies that leads to damaging the small intestine's lining and hindering it from absorbing nutrients. Typical complications from celiac disease include fatigue, bloating, anemia, diarrhea, and weight loss.

There is currently no cure. For those who've been diagnosed with it, eliminating gluten from their diet is imperative. Doctors also typically recommend gluten-free diets for any patients they've diagnosed as being gluten-intolerant. Gluten-free means no bread, pasta, salad dressing, beer, soy sauce, french fries, and the list goes on. In 2013, to help consumers living with celiac disease and gluten sensitivities, the FDA added gluten content labeling to the Food Allergen Labeling and Consumer Protection Act of 2004.

Yet, I consider some of this to also be mythical in regards to adhering to a gluten-free diet when not having been formally diagnosed with celiac disease or gluten intolerance. Many people "symptom-shop" online, diagnose themselves to have these conditions, and limit themselves to gluten-free diets because "gluten-free" is a popular trend.

According to Harry Balzer of the American market research company NPD Group, 29 percent of Americans are currently trying to reduce their gluten intake or avoid gluten completely, while, again, only about one percent of Americans suffer from celiac disease. There seems to be a growing misconception that "gluten-free" and "healthier" are synonymous, with growth in the global market for gluten-free products projected to rise from approximately 2.8 billion US dollars in 2015 to over 7.5 billion dollars by 2024.

Americans have embraced a lot of diet crazes in the past sixty years: high-protein/low carbs, food combining, and fat-free to name just a few. Sadly, as with so many of these crazes, the current gluten-free one is inspiring a lot of people to eliminate whole categories of foods from their diet. In the meantime, they're ignoring nutritious grains like corn, oats, buckwheat, sorghum, and many others that do not contain gluten. Despite the fact that they don't have celiac disease or gluten intolerance, wheat becomes their enemy with one result being deprivation of a lot of important nutrients.

Yes, there are adult-onset allergies, but the dramatic symptoms of a genuine, genetic gluten allergy start manifesting long before adulthood. Most of the time, these individuals' allergies and stomach problems are caused by inflammation in the digestive system. So they turn to white bread instead, regardless of its alarmingly high content of sugar and its nutritional wasteland for reasons we've already discussed, and to processed white flour, which has had most of its fiber and nutrients removed during processing.

Whereas complex breads and brown breads contain valuable nutrients such as fiber, calcium, iron, potassium, and folate. Eliminate those breads and you also eliminate vital protein, vitamins, minerals, and fiber so important for good gut bacteria.

Another myth that has become widely accepted in the anti-gluten fad is that a gluten-free diet energizes the metabolism. After extensive research among nutritionists and other biochemical specialists, including at the University of Wisconsin's School of Public Health, not a single study has found any validity to that claim. Gluten takes no more energy to digest than countless other natural food compounds. In fact, the body can digest many foods containing gluten more quickly than it can digest most animal proteins.

In conclusion, before you make any dramatic dietary changes, don't let your friends or yoga classmates or two-hour anti-gluten seminar or Dr. Google decide whether or not you're gluten-intolerant. Your physician can conduct screenings to determine your body's reaction to gluten. It makes more sense to know for sure before you eliminate vital nutrients from your diet.

If you have a sensitive digestive system, you can start some of your own screening by eliminating nutritionally worthless, potentially inflammatory foods from your diet. Those containing an excess of processed white flour and sugar in particular are often the cause of inflammation, fatigue, and bloating, and the diseases they lead to. Sugar and processed foods can do much more damage than gluten can for those who haven't been diagnosed with celiac disease or gluten intolerance. It's essential to be well-informed, especially when information is so accessible. To be informed is to be healthy.

Chapter Eight

Life after I Quit Caffeine & Alcohol

"First, do no harm"
— Hippocrates

A lot of articles make claims like, "Adding these three foods to your diet will enhance your life, beauty, and longevity." Unfortunately, there is no miracle food that will enhance your life if you're eating it with one hand, while diminishing your life eating something harmful with the other. There is no miracle food that can instantly reverse the damage you might be doing to your body every day.

We all want healthy bodies, and there are plenty of foods and supplements that can help make that happen over time. But first, we have to stop destroying our bodies. Let's start by talking about coffee. The smell of a fresh cup can be a pleasant, inviting aroma that affects our mood and makes us feel warm, while picturesque adjectives and introspective poems further enhance the comforts it gives. So why on earth did I give it up, and why would you be wise to do the same?

People mistakenly believe that coffee is what gives them the energy they need to make it through their day. The truth is, caffeine in coffee is a stimulant that affects the central nervous system and wakes us up, it doesn't energize us up. It "pulls the trigger" on our bodies to speed up the release of cortisol, a hormone that intensifies our physiological stress responses which we rely on to make us react quickly when we're in life-threatening situations.

Caffeine ratchets up the heart rate, elevates blood pressure, and increases muscle tension. It forces our bodies to use their own surges of energy in a very short period of time; and in the wake of that surge, our mood, hyper-alertness, and energy collapse a couple of hours afterward, commonly leading to headaches, indigestion, and lethargy, and to us believing that what we need is another shot of stimulant. It also blocks the effectiveness of adenosine, a natural chemical in our cells that alerts the body that it needs rest. If used regularly, caffeine can cause a mild physical dependence. Giving it up "cold turkey" can even trigger withdrawal symptoms such as headaches, depression, fatigue, anxiety, and impaired concentration.

It's also found in black and green teas, colas, chocolates, over-the-counter medications such as diet pills, pain relievers and cough syrups, and energy bars and drinks (usually in the form of an additive called guarana).

I strongly advocate eliminating all sources of caffeine from your life, but I'm enough of a realist to know that some of you would rather leap off the nearest roof (which should give you a hint that you might be more dependent on it than you realize). If you insist on clinging to your caffeine habit, here are a few tips I hope you'll keep in mind:

Moderation is essential. According to the FDA, if you're a healthy adult, not pregnant, and have no liver issues, 400 milligrams of caffeine a day should be your absolute maximum. More than that can put you at risk for the common side effects of headaches, nausea, anxiety, and interrupted sleep patterns.

Switching to decaffeinated coffee after a certain hour of the day can help normalize your sleep patterns and can even be useful in weaning you off of your coffee habit. However, it's also important to understand that decaffeinated coffee isn't really caffeine-free. The amount varies from one brand to the next, but on average, an eight-ounce cup of decaffeinated coffee is likely to contain seven milligrams of caffeine, compared to an eight-ounce cup of regular caffeinated coffee, which typically contains a minimum of eighty-five milligrams. So, if you have your heart set on saying goodbye to caffeine, remember there's a difference between "decaf" and "no-caf."

It can take several weeks for a heavy caffeine user to detox from it. Drinking lots of water and herbal tea will help. But in the long run, your heart, blood pressure, nervous system, and stress levels will be so grateful, not to mention all the nights of good, sound, restful sleep you'll enjoy once you've put caffeine behind you.

The better alternative for upping our energy is through diet and exercise. That way keeps us going at a healthy, steady pace without putting our bodies through a stimulant-induced pattern of harmful hormonal surges and slumps. My studies at an herbal medicine school in Malibu, California helped me discover more about these healthy alternatives to support and increase my energy. Cacao, for example, is a great source of energy, as are certain teas.

In case you're not familiar with cacao, it's derived from the same seeds as those that create cocoa, cocoa butter, and chocolate. Cocoa has been popular since ancient times, prized for its magical smell, high energy value and high vibrations, and for its suitability as a traditional ceremonial drink to celebrate special occasions like the birth of a baby or the launch of a new endeavor. There's even a legend in which the first woman on earth appeared from a cocoa bean that fell to the ground, suggesting a connection with yin, the feminine energy in all of us.

I often think of this history as I prepare my own hot cacao drinks. It's part of a special tradition every morning. It's a time when I look forward with gratitude to the new day ahead supported by the exquisite cacao aroma that helps keep me grounded and present.

I grind fifteen cacao beans and add them to two cups of simmering water. I add one tablespoon of cacao nibs, one inch of vanilla bean or one teaspoon of vanilla extract, and let the mixture simmer for thirteen minutes while I set aside a pot and add one teaspoon of cacao butter. I let it sit for a couple of minutes in the pot, pass it through a strainer, and then it's wonderfully ready for me to drink two cups. I like my cocoa drink with coconut milk. I sweeten mine with two tablespoons of maple syrup, or you can add your own natural sweetener if you like. Between the quiet, special ritual I've made around preparing it, irresistible fragrance, and taste that's been cele brated for thousands of years, I can't honestly say I miss coffee. Cocoa is a source for steady long-lasting energy.

Another great alternative to coffee which boosts the energy, immune and vascular systems, as well as reduces inflammation and muscle pain, is ginger allspice tea. For two cups of tea, I stir two full tablespoons of fresh ground ginger into 3 1/5 cups of boiling water and simmer for five minutes. Then I add a small pinch of nutmeg, four whole dry cloves, one cinnamon stick, two small pinches of cardamom, and seven whole pieces of Jamaican allspice. I simmer that mixture for eight minutes, turn off the flame, cover, and let steep for ten more minutes. Then, I pour it through a strainer, add two or three tablespoons of maple syrup and a squeeze of fresh lemon, and enjoy. I prefer it strong, but if it's too strong and spicy for you, you can always add water to dilute it more. Natural sweeteners are optional. Ginger allspice tea makes me feel warm, alert, and ready for the day, much more than coffee ever did.

An occasional cup of coffee as a treat won't do much harm, though it's still important to appreciate it as a special drink that can help us heal our past abusive relationships with caffeine. Just drinking coffee on "automatic" mode and skipping the part about appreciation takes away some of the pleasure. Overconsumption may also be linked to many diseases and accelerated aging, and its high acidity may affect the body on a cellular level.

A second thing I strongly suggest eliminating is alcohol. It is the most commonly used legal drug in the world. Alcohol is so available and so affordable that we rarely think twice about introducing it into our lives. But you'll be pleasantly surprised by the results if you give it up for even just thirty days. Physically, you'll find a reduction in skin swelling and redness, and very probably lose weight too. Mentally, you'll find your mind is clearer, you're more emotionally stable, and more motivated and productive. Financially, you'll save money. And in the bigger picture, according to research by Dr. Richard de Visser from the University of Sussex, giving up alcohol for a month will help reduce the number of drinking days in your later years.

No one likes alcohol the first time they try it. That's because our bodies are telling us that something isn't right. But we ignore those signals, excuse them with the mythical age-old cliché that "it's an acquired flavor," and try masking the ugly taste and odor with soft drinks, juices and mixers. Before long, we become so accustomed to our alcoholic beverages that we start enjoying them and giving them credit for all the fun we have at parties, and come to a point where we can't imagine enjoying a party without them.

As our "social drinking" continues, our self-protective bodies build up a tolerance to the toxic substances, and inevitably we end up needing more and more alcohol to give us that relaxed feeling that attracted us to it in the first place. "More and more" can easily lead to addiction, often without our even realizing it's happening.

It's a common misconception that if you don't get drunk to the point of occasional blackouts, or you can function for a few days at a time without a drink, then you don't have an alcohol problem. But the truth is, because there are many levels of alcoholism, there are also many alcoholics who are convinced they're not addicted at all. Now that I'm in my early forties, I've come to realize with sadness just how many people I know who are close to middle age and act helpless about stopping alcohol from harming their bodies and personalities. Instead, they seem to accept of it as a part of their nature. Functioning alcoholics have almost become the norm in our society. Many of them claim that a glass or two of red wine a day can help them slow down their aging process, which is absurd—there is absolutely no health benefit to daily intoxication.

Alcoholism can also sneak up on anyone who drinks to alleviate stress or emotional pain, or just to unwind after a long day. Although it may seem at the time as if they're "taking a fun break from their problems," really they're adding a whole new problem to their list; becoming dependent on alcohol on top of everything else they're going through. Once the body has become addicted to alcohol, it's more vulnerable to a long list of serious diseases that affect the brain, nerves, muscle tissue, heart, liver, pancreas, and other organs. It's also more vulnerable to an increased risk of cancer, anxiety, and sleeplessness, not to mention the telltale haggard look of puffy red skin and under-eye bags.

Compounding the downside of drinking alcohol is the vicious cycle withdrawal can create. If addiction has set in and the body has become accustomed to functioning with alcohol in its system, giving it up is likely to trigger headaches, nausea, anxiety, and a number of other withdrawal symptoms which can easily lead to reaching for alcohol again to relieve those symptoms. Thus, the destructive cycle can keep going on and on.

The best idea is to not start drinking at all. But most of us started consuming alcohol when we were young. Between movies and the adults around us, it looked fun, normal, socially desirable, even elegant and an attribute for getting along in our culture. That alcohol also happened to be psychologically and physically addictive was beside the point, if even mentioned at all. Now as adults we each have our own choices to make, choices no one else can make for us. In regards to alcohol, the choice is whether to let this drug destroy our bodies or to keep our bodies happy and healthy.

Research also shows that consistent consumption of alcohol reduces our brain gray matter and weakens our connection to our Higher Selves. It lowers our vibrations and weakens our immune system, too.

Working with herbs in traditional medicine, I gained an understanding of how alcohol operates on an energetic level. Alcohol is used in preparing tinctures. The process involves capturing the essence of herbs, which in addition to their chemical components, they also have their own unique vibrational fields, or the soul of the plant. Alcohol helps extract them. The same thing happens when a person experiences alcohol-induced blackouts. In that case, the soul can't handle the intoxication of the body and minimizes its energetic presence by reducing its vibrations.

Not many people understand that the buzz they get from alcohol is a by-product of the direct intoxication of the body. It's not written on those bottles that you're going to pay for your fun with possible diseases and addiction. It's also not a secret that alcohol sales create thriving businesses. It's the most available drug and the most dangerous one, too. In fact, the

Global Communication on Drug Policy reports that alcohol is the most harmful drug, followed by heroin and cocaine.

Giving up alcohol may sound impossible, especially if you are addicted to it. But alcoholism is not a prison, and quitting is very possible with qualified help readily available if you need it. You can improve your life in millions of ways by becoming alcohol-free. Within a few short weeks of quitting, you'll start feeling significantly better. Everyone deserves to enjoy their life and be given a chance for the best life experience.

Chapter Nine

Better Sleep, Better Life
Deep Sleep, Its Benefits, & Tips on How to Achieve It

"Early to bed, early to rise makes a man healthy, wealthy and wise."
— Benjamin Franklin

We established in the previous chapter that caffeine and alcohol can interfere with our sleep patterns, which makes it even more important that we eliminate them from our lives. We also know how much better we feel after a good night's sleep, yet a new study by the Centers for Disease Control and Prevention indicates that around 35 percent of American adults routinely fall short of the recommended seven to nine hours of rest per night.

There are many reasons to include quality sleep in your health and wellness priority list. Our bodies and minds actually accomplish a lot while we're sleeping and "out of the way" for several hours. Toxins in the brain that accumulate during our waking hours are removed while we sleep. During sleep, the immune system releases cytokines, proteins produced by our cells, that help regulate the body's response to disease, infection, inflammation, and trauma. In fact, sleep has such an important effect on the body's organs and systems that a chronic lack of it increases the risk of disorders including high blood pressure, diabetes, heart disease, and obesity.

One of the many hormones released while we sleep is melatonin. It regulates our circadian rhythm, also known as our sleep/wake cycle. The release of melatonin increases during the middle two hours of sleep. Its antioxidant properties benefit us in many ways. For example, it facilitates the skin repairing itself from the damage and pollutants subjected to during waking hours. In other words, there's a very real, very practical reason for the term "beauty sleep."

Our levels of the stress hormone cortisol decrease the most during the final three hours of sleep, which is another reason why our skin suffers when we're sleep-deprived. A lack of sleep and the resulting increase in cortisol adds stress to our bodies; cortisol is an enemy of collagen, a protein in the body that, among many other functions, maintains the elasticity and firmness of the skin.

It's also during sleep that our sympathetic nervous system has a chance to relax. That means the body's internal fight-or-flight response gets a much-needed break. It stands to reason then that when our fight-or-flight instinct is consistently deprived of regular, reliable opportunities to "stand down," health concerns like high blood pressure and high cholesterol are bound to increase.

Our minds and emotions are every bit as dependent on good sleep habits as our bodies. Our brains use sleep hours to process the information we've gathered during the day, filing some of it away for future reference and discarding some of it as trivia. The words "let me sleep on it" are perfectly legitimate. Sometimes during sleep we come up with the solution to a problem we've been struggling with. Sometimes we wake up realizing that something that seemed like a big deal the night before is really no big deal at all. Sometimes our minds "let off steam" by acting out in the form of seemingly meaningless and chaotic dreams, the frustration, confusion, disappointment, or nonsense we've experienced. This processing of the day's information is especially essential in creating our long-term memories, none of which would be possible without a good night's sleep.

The sleep cycle can be summarized as this: When we begin to fall asleep but are still somewhat awake, the small, rapid beta waves the brain starts producing gradually calm to slower alpha waves. Stage 1 of the normal sleep cycle begins when we're actually asleep. It usually lasts about ten minutes and is marked by the brain's creation of slow, meditative, high-amplitude theta waves.

During Stage 2, which lasts around twenty minutes, the brain produces short bursts of activity called "sleep spindles," named for the image they create when monitored by an electroencephalogram (EEG). They help us ignore external stimuli, which is why during Stage 2 we're less likely to be awakened than during Stage 1.

Slow, deep delta waves are a phenomenon of Stages 3 and 4, the deepest sleep, the first episode of which generally lasts from forty-five to ninety minutes. We usually experience sleep Stages 3 and 4, also known as Delta Sleep, several times a night. It's during these stages when we're least aware of, and least responsive to, our surroundings, thus most resistant to being woken up. This is the body's refreshing, restorative, regenerative period as the human growth hormone that promotes cell repair is released. It's also believed by some neuroscientists that this phase of the sleep cycle helps clear the brain so it can receive new information the next day.

Deep sleep is undoubtedly the most mysterious phase of the sleep cycle. It's when we disengage almost completely from our environment. It's when we experience the most essential physical and mental restoration we count on. One of the many benefits of meditation is that the restorative delta waves of these sleep stages can also be achieved during a deep meditative state. It's also during Stages 3 and 4 that our sleep cycle is most susceptible to stress, aging, drugs, and a variety of other harms. If you wake up feeling run down and unrested, it's very likely that you didn't get enough deep sleep during the night.

Having a greater understanding of our bodies and the different levels of body/spirit relationships has more benefits than we can even imagine. For instance, science seems to have gone as far as it can now to unveil what's happening with our consciousness while we're sleeping. Instead, we are having to look for some answers in spiritual knowledge.

According to cosmology, we live in a world of duality and impermanence, a world of happiness and sadness, sickness and health, disappointments and victories, the heat of summers and the cold of winters. However, at least one exception is the state of deep sleep through which we can access non-dual perception.

One of the world's most ancient Indian spiritual scriptures called the Upanishads explains the mystery of deep sleep by describing what we experience as another state of being in addition to active-waking and dreaming states. This state of deep sleep is the third state in which we experience nothingness. What the Upanishads explain is a deep philosophy that tells us we're not limited by our bodies, rather we're an awareness that experiences three different states of life. That deep sleep is not an absence of experience, but an experience of nothingness. And that our active and sleeping worlds are unreal and do not have intrinsic qualities from our consciousness.

Further, when we awaken and are fairly certain it was us who experienced an active dream state, and the nothingness of a deep sleep, our higher immortal self is at work observing our wide-awake activities and our sleeping state. The topic of sleep is not completely incomprehensible for us; however, we still do not know the all-important answer to why we spend one-third of our lives asleep. Every night, we dive into the realm of our thoughts, memories, and emotions while cutting off the external physical world. Deep sleep offers its own proof that we're not limited to our bodies, and that we can exist free of any activities including our thoughts and emotions. We're bigger than these. We are an eternal consciousness able to observe different states of our existence.

Another important aspect of sleep is the daytime nap. Napping can be very helpful when you overuse your personal computer, your brain. Researchers have found that a midday nap can improve our brain's efficiency and help us sort through unconscious information we've taken in without necessarily realizing it, similar to how nighttime sleeping does.

You'll understand the fascinating work of brain waves when you read the upcoming chapter "Brain Waves and Why They Matter." But for this discussion, it's worth noting that while a brief midday nap of twenty to twenty-five minutes isn't a viable replacement for meditation, it does provide the same valuable function of slowing down brain waves from their wide-awake highly active state to being more moderate and restorative.

Though there's no way to guarantee a good night's sleep that includes an adequate amount of deep sleep, below are some reliable tips to significantly improve your sleep habits:

- Practice deep breathing and other relaxation techniques immediately before your bedtime to help reduce stress, a barrier to deep sleep.

- Whenever possible, go to bed and wake up at the same time each day of the week, rather than at any time you feel like it.

- Make sure your bedroom is kept at a temperature of between 66 to 72 degrees Fahrenheit. If your room is too warm, it can interfere with your body's ability to induce a deeper, more consistent sleep, which studies have found occurs more reliably when your core temperature is cooler. Also, a study by the National Institute of Health has demonstrated that sleeping in a cool room can help burn more calories and stimulate your metabolism by increasing levels of "brown fat," a type of fat that is triggered when the body gets cold.

- Make sure your bedroom is dark enough to encourage your body's natural release of melatonin. According to multiple recent studies, there is a phenomenon called "iPad insomnia," which refers to the blue light emanating from electronic screens—cell phones, computers, laptops, iPads, et cetera. This specific frequency of light throws off the body's biological clock and interrupts the circadian rhythm. Thus, it is strongly recommended to turn off all electronic devices, including your TV, at least one to two hours before bedtime.

- Create a relaxation routine before you go to bed. This could include a warm saltwater bath, reading, a stroll in fresh air, a cup of chamomile tea, or anything that helps your body and mind wind down. This also means disconnecting from emails, voicemails, text messages, and social media, as well as refraining from exercise, caffeine, and alcohol several hours before bedtime.

- If you have trouble falling asleep or you wake up during the night and cannot go back to sleep, don't lie awake in bed as it's likely to make you anxious that you're not sleeping. Instead, get up and repeat some part of your relaxation ritual, whether it's reading, or listening to music, or having another cup of chamomile tea, until you feel a sense of sleep coming on again.

Take your sleeping habits as seriously as you take your other health concerns. If sleep disruption becomes chronic, or if you don't feel refreshed and re-energized upon waking, it's a good idea to consult with your doctor. Most sleep disorders can be dealt with effectively, so don't write them off as normal, or hopeless. Quality sleep is not one of life's luxuries, it's a requirement.

Chapter Ten

Fascia & Yoga
New Importance of an Ancient Practice

If you've never heard the word "fascia," you're not alone. It's one of the most often overlooked parts of the human body, and also one of the most essential. Fascia is a three-dimensional web of thin, fibrous, densely woven connective tissue that extends throughout head to toe. It accounts for approximately 20 percent of our body mass, encasing and infusing every one of our internal organs—every muscle, bone, nerve, blood vessel, and artery. It surrounds the trillions of cells in our bodies. It is flexible and able to adjust to our every move, and contributes to making us one integrated organism as opposed to a collection of separate body parts. Blood, water, and nutrients circulate to our cells through these webs of fascia, webs that deliver the nourishment our cells need and then washes away the waste. Fascia is an important factor in our ability to recover from injuries and disabilities, and is essential to both our movement and physical stability every day of our lives.

A common way to picture fascia is to imagine several strands of string, each strand secured in cling wrap. Then imagine those strands bundled together and secured with another layer of cling wrap. Gather dozens of those bundles into one, secure this larger bundle with cling wrap and you have a primitive model of the way muscles are structured, with fascia being the cling wrap that holds them together.

In fact, next time you buy a raw chicken breast at the grocery store, take a moment before you prepare it to notice the fine, filmy layer on the top in between the skin and the meat. That filmy layer is fascia, and the chicken breast example is an excellent way to view two of the three kinds of fascia in our bodies: The superficial fascia close to the skin, and the deep fascia that surrounds our bones and muscles. The third kind, visceral fascia, surrounds our organs.

Fascia consists of collagen, which gives support to our bones and muscles; elastin, a "shock absorber" that allows our muscles to stretch; and a transparent gelatinous component called "ground substance" that allows our muscle fibers to glide over each other without resistance. It's obviously crucial to our physical structure and overall health, and it's just as crucial that we take good care of it. If fascia becomes dry and dense, it can't perform its circulatory functions efficiently. Toxins can become trapped, leading to potential infections and diseases that can, among other things, restrict our mobility.

There are two ways to promote healthy fascia and therefore promote our wellness in general: hydration and movement. The importance of generally keeping our bodies hydrated is well known, but a lesser known, more specific reason is to keep the fascia healthy. Water is essential to the fascial network's elasticity, suppleness, and lubrication. In fact, one of the many consequences of dried-out superficial fascia is that it can tighten, become distorted, and begin puckering the skin into a form known as cellulite. So, drinking more water is always recommended. Regular soft-tissue massages can also be enormously helpful in distributing water and other natural bodily fluids throughout the fascial network.

The fascial network also relies on us to *move*. We sit at our work desks for hours at a time. We sit in our cars commuting for hours at a time. We sit on our sofas watching TV for hours at a time. Even when we think we're resting by sitting during those times, we're usually holding in situational tension and chronic stress.

Inactivity and stress are guaranteed to harden and freeze fascia. However, getting in the habit of moving, stretching and doing simple exercises throughout the day can make a noticeable difference in overall wellness within just a few short weeks. But if you really want to make your fascia, connective tissue in general, and your whole body happy, you can do what I've done— fall in love with yoga.

Yoga is one example of a practice that's particularly beneficial to our fascial network, and in general to our mental and physical well-being. That's because our fascia also stores our psychological and physiological trauma. Yoga has been a popular, effective discipline since 3,000 BCE, which makes it difficult to deny its profound, life-changing effects. Along with hydration and other healthy lifestyle choices, yoga, especially slow yoga like Yin Yoga that offers deeper access to the body's functioning, transforms the fascial network. Tom Myers, author of the book *Anatomy Trains,* brings up another fascinating aspect of the yoga/yoga therapy/fascia connection. He points out that the nervous, circulatory, and fascial systems are all interconnected and interdependent, so changing the fascial system changes the whole body.

An example he uses is depression. It can be treated psychologically. It can be treated chemically. But Tom Myers suggests it can also be treated through yoga's unique ability to impact and change the fascial network. He explains that a person suffering from depression typically has a compromised posture with their shoulders rounded, chest compressed, head downward and spine curved. Since the body takes on a specific, identifiable shape and form, and fascia is the organ of form, he concludes that the fascial network and other connective tissue is where significant changes need to be made. When the fascia improves, breathing improves. When breathing improves, the body's chemistry improves. When the chemistry improves, the mind improves. And it's all possible thanks to the miraculous transformations yoga offers for people of every age, size, shape, and skill level.

In addition to enhancing the health of the complex fascial network, yoga provides a number of other long-lasting, life-changing benefits. Many people sign up for yoga classes in order to become stronger, look better, and fight the loss of muscle mass and changes in posture that come with aging. But they end up staying with it because they find it both a rejuvenating physical activity and a remarkable enhancer of their mental and emotional well-being. Yoga practitioners call it "increasing space inside the body."

It does this by unblocking energy channels through various poses that change the flow of blood and energy throughout the body. And it stretches the muscles and spine to create more space between the vertebrae. Because it promotes better posture, it also creates more space for our vital organs. Furthermore, it focuses our attention on deep breathing, which cleanses, heals, and eases stress to create more space for new attitudes and perspectives, which in turn dislodges imprinted traumatic experiences and clears the way for transforming ourselves from victim to victor.

Yoga has also expanded my consciousness about the beauty of human proportion. The fascinating truth is that those proportions are equal to the well-known golden ratio of Fibonacci, most commonly known by Leonardo da Vinci's stunning celebration of those proportions in his 1490 drawing *The Vitruvian Man* and the body's divine connection to everything in existence through the geometrical laws known as sacred geometry.

Sacred geometry is a code of creation. Everything in nature is made up of a proportional formula that is repeated everywhere from flower petals, to creatures of the sea, to the phalanges of our fingers, to the unique beauty of every face, to the magnificent patterns of the universe, and to all points in between. Since geometry and mathematical ratios are consistent in all of creation, it reminds us that we are part of a blessed whole, and that the science of mathematics was discovered, not created, by humankind. Yoga postures, or asanas, create geometrical forms that help increase vibratory frequencies and bring us to deeper meditative states.

Yoga has made an extraordinary difference in my life, physically, mentally, and emotionally. Countless insights and pathways of learning have opened up to me because of it, ones I might have otherwise gone through life unaware of. I hope you'll try yoga if you already haven't. It won't take long for you to understand why it's been around for thousands of years and grows more popular every day.

Part One

Conclusion

Following our discussion on our physical energy center, our lower Sun, and how to develop it by improving our diets and exercise regimens, you can now better understand how your body knows to operate through its own intelligence, without your control. As we all know, the first rule of communication is to learn to listen. This same rule applies to our relationship with our bodies. We have to be receptive and listen.

We can't ingest anything without paying attention to the direct response it has on our bodies. They complain to us through allergies, pain, insomnia, blue circles under the eyes, fatigue, and digestive problems. So rather than eating just out of habit, we must instead learn to ask ourselves whether those things we find tasty will bring our bodies benefit or harm. We have good reason to do this and to make friends with our bodies.

A healthy lifestyle begins with what we eat, because a healthy digestive system is a cornerstone of health. Over 75 percent of our immune cells live within the intestinal tract, and one of the most important energy centers, our third Sun, is located in the abdominal area. The ancient Chinese self-healing practice of Chi Gun considers this area, which they call the lower dantian, to be one of the most vital parts of the body and the source of our internal energy. Western scientists support this concept, calling the gut our "second brain." The ancient Greek physician Hippocrates, an iconic figure in the history of medicine, concurred with his observation that "all disease begins in the gut."

We already know this intuitively. So often, when in pain, we put our hands on our stomachs. Pay attention to that part of your body. Mentally build your connection to it. Rub your palms together and place them on your stomach. Feel the heat. Send it your kindness and a smile, and feel the response.

We need to remember that our bodies are intricate conglomerations of living beings, all of which produce, and are sensitive to, resonant vibrations and frequencies. An essential part of taking care of our health involves maintaining our highest possible vibrations and avoiding low-vibration foods that compromise our bodies' frequencies and immune systems.

We need to conduct regular audits and analyze the food we eat, and build in periodic changes. Start recording what you ingest every day, including beverages, and then analyze your diet each week. Note the percentage of harmful foods you consume (those with low vibrational frequencies such as processed food, sugar, sodas, and white flour products) and your percentage of wholesome natural foods (those with high vibrational frequencies such as fruits, vegetables, and healthy food you prepare at home).

Note how much pure water you drink.

Be sure to set attainable goals for your diet by taking small steps. If the food you're consuming doesn't seem or feel healthy to you based on the "feedback" you're getting from your body, then reduce it. Get rid of processed foods and packaged products. Try cooking at home more, or at least pay more attention to what's in the food when you go out to eat. Try adding probiotic-rich fermented foods to your diet, drinking more pure water, starting each day with freshly squeezed lemon juice in a glass of warm water, and reducing your consumption of sugar, red meat, dairy products, coffee, and alcohol.

Bring more exercise and sports activities into your life, and add some stretching or yoga.

Pay attention to your posture. The spine is the structure holding your whole organism, and it must be straight. Strengthen your spinal muscles with special exercises or long walks. As Eastern wisdom tells us, "If there is a choice between lying or sitting, choose to sit. If there is a choice between sitting or standing, choose to stand. If there is a choice between standing or walking, go."

Be outside as much as you can because nature is healing.

Remember that you are made of light. All life on earth uses sunlight to sustain itself and to grow. Absolutely everything we eat, whether it's a plant or an animal, owes its existence to the sun. Through the food we consume, we absorb sunlight that has been modified by an invisible light. Ultimately this light is *us*. Recognize and embrace your exceptional human nature and you'll find yourself making choices based on what's best for you.

Eliminate judgements and comparisons when it comes to your body, and in general. Start by being kind to yourself. Look in the mirror with a kind and compassionate smile. Appreciate your body.

Love yourself.

PART 2

THE MENTAL
ENERGY CENTER

Our upper Sun, or energy center, is connected to one of the most important and mysterious organs in our bodies—the brain. How this incredibly complicated organ works, how and why our minds can be our best friends or our worst enemies, and how we can learn to reprogram them so that we can manage our thoughts rather than them managing us is a lifelong pursuit.

What makes each of us unique from everyone else on earth is our own experiences—experiences that shape our thoughts and reactions whether we're aware of them or not. Experience doesn't just come from the lives we're living now, because our true Nature, our divine essence, always was and always will be immortal and infinite. So when we reincarnate and physically manifest ourselves in this world, we bring with us the memories and experiences, deeds, thoughts, emotions, and lessons we've learned in every lifetime we've ever lived. To understand where all that information is stored and how it becomes the filter through which our five senses perceive the world, we have to merge science and spirituality.

Sigmund Freud, founding father of psychoanalysis, called this storehouse the unconscious mind. Yogic teachings call it the subtle body, visible to some in the form of an aura that emanates from, and surrounds all, living things. Christianity calls it the soul.

Knowing that we have more than one physical body helps us understand that our emotional and mental centers, invisible to the naked eye and made of energy, don't die when our physical bodies do. In terms of modern science, the energy just changes forms. It can neither be created nor destroyed and thus continues after the death of the physical body. Although the emotional and mental centers are often mistaken for our Higher Self, our emotional and mental centers are still only layers of our true Higher Self, not the Higher Self itself.

Every time we reincarnate from a past life, that vast amount of experience comes with us ready for the new lifetime ahead with more lessons to be learned and stored. I believe in reincarnation because of my own experience. After I gave birth to my first child, I asked the doctors to let me visit her in a special room in the hospital where all newborn babies who needed extra care were. All were born on the same day, but all were very different. One was very upset. Another was so happy to lie under a bright yellow lamp.

One baby had such a serious expression that there was no doubt he was processing some important information. Another looked very sad and tired, as if thinking to himself, "Here we go again."

It was visibly apparent that each baby came with its own "baggage" and that each of their souls arrived with different experiences. I spent some time in that room watching the newborns. What I saw gave me confirmation that we come into this world already being who we are, and that this life is not our first one.

Our conscious minds have no direct access to the information in our unconscious minds. That information can only be communicated through our subconscious minds via hypnosis or advanced meditation. However, we do receive messages every second from our unconscious minds by way of our thoughts and reactions as perceived through our five senses. That information is registered by the conscious mind, absorbed and reacted to by the subconscious, before moving even deeper into the unconscious where it triggers information that's already stored. It then transmits both positive and negative reactions to the conscious mind again. In other words, those thoughts that constantly bubble up in your conscious mind according to your previous experiences build new experiences and reactions that are then imprinted again in your unconscious.

So just as there are no two identical lifetime experiences from this life and past lives, there are no two identical views about the world. We each perceive things differently, and therefore we react to them differently.

Scientific opinion suggests that thoughts are a part of the material world, that they're a chemical reaction in our brains generated by neurons. The spiritual point of view, in response, counters with a question: If our consciousness is just the product of chemical reactions in our brains, where did it get its first experience? Where did our awareness come from?

The answer is: It was always there. It wasn't created at the same time as our bodies. It has been embodied, which means our minds are infinitely more complex and fascinating than we tend to appreciate. Though we can have much more control over them than we tend to believe—peace of mind really is within our reach.

For example, I've learned to stop looking "out there" for peace of mind and realize that the answers are "in here" instead, and that they really are accessible if I know where and how to find them.

Chapter Eleven

Modern Challenges

Before the development of modern technologies during the past century, people lived with a different rhythm than we do now. Once upon a time, people lived in harmony with nature and with the land they cultivated. Our ancestors communicated more with each other by working in teams, not according to time frames, reports, and schedules. They lived in small, familiar communities, passing each other with a smile and a greeting. Most of the time, stress was an occasional phenomenon caused only by a life-threatening situation. In those instances, stress hormones were instinctively released to focus all the body's energy and attention on survival enabling it to perform beyond its normal capabilities to escape danger. When the threat had passed, the body's mechanisms returned to normal.

Today we live in a society of strangers, physically surrounded by people but not connected with them emotionally; and our bodies experience stressful autonomic reactions to fear every day. Unfortunately, while those reactions serve us well for short periods of time in crisis situations, they've become chronic for most of us. Stress has become so common, it's almost accepted as the way we're meant to live. But that can't be the case because pervasive stress has a direct negative impact on our health and quality of life. It destroys the immune system, the nervous system, the vascular system, the digestive system, and every other system in the body.

We fear the future. We regret the past. As a result, a large part of our society either suffers from depression and anxiety, which corresponds to fears about tomorrow or subconscious regrets about yesterday. For thousands of years, people lived simply and in approximate equality, passing almost the same tools of labor and life from one generation to the next. Then electricity was invented and people's lives changed dramatically. Living in big cities became more attractive and society in general became more interested in convenience and progress. By the time the information age of today took over, making life even easier and gratification more immediate, the living conditions of an ordinary Westerner could be equated to the privileged life of some European medieval prince.

Unfortunately, we don't have the luxury of regarding all these amazing, relatively recent developments as free. We pay for them dearly every day with stress, anxiety, depression, and chronic disease. We were unprepared for such quick, dramatic changes in our lives, especially when they've been compounded by ancient human addictions that devolved into new ones such as alcohol, tobacco, coffee, sugar, prescription painkillers, social networking, and more.

For better or worse, social media specifically, and the internet in general, have become mirrors of our society. We must take a long, honest look at the wholeness reflected and accept it in its entirety, without selectivity. Once we admit our mistakes and accept the weaknesses staring back at us in the mirror, we can correct them and grow.

We have to admit, for example, that social media creates an unhealthy competition, a constant tendency to compare ourselves to others and to feel inferior if we don't have as much money or followers, or if it looks as if everyone else is having more fun than we are. People aren't inclined to post their failures and mistakes online. Very few of them will publicly announce, "I mourned yesterday," or, "I had a job interview but was turned down," or, "I'm sitting here depressed and alone with a bottle of vodka." A friend recently confessed to me that every time he checks his Insta-feed, he feels like a complete loser, wondering why all the Instagram users he follows have such bright, busy, interesting lives compared to his. I applaud the Instagram initiative to hide "likes" from profile pages. Those "likes" illuminate the unhealthy competition and fears our younger generation is so vulnerable to. After all, the goal of communication is to share your experience through the unique prism of your personality, not to satisfy an urge to be validated by strangers.

We're setting unreachable and exaggerated standards for ourselves, for each other, and for our children, and in the process, digging ourselves into a rut. For the first time in history, human life expectancy has decreased. We're raising the unhealthiest generation of children, and we've lost track of our most authentic priorities. Our thoughts tend to lead us into anxiety and depression, we've stopped listening to our bodies, and our emotions seem to have more control over us than we have over them. We think one thing, we feel another, and we end up doing a third.

Life feels chaotic. We've lost our inner unity of mind, body, and soul and lost our sacred connection to nature. We are not separate creatures on this planet, we are one with every living thing, which means that when we diminish our planet, we diminish ourselves. The earth is rich with energy that can rejuvenate us and center us if we'll only open ourselves to it again, cherish it, and make a habit of renewing our sacred relationship with it.

In fact, spending time in nature is also referred to as "taking a nature pill." For decades, scientists have been trying to establish a dosage for the "nature pill" that will make a genuine difference in our health and stress levels, and still fit comfortably into our daily lives. It looks as if they've finally succeeded. A study called "Urban Nature Experiences Reduce Stress in the Context of Daily Life Based on Salivary Biomarkers" was published in the journal *Frontiers in Psychology* (Hunter et al. 2019). The conclusion, according to lead authors MaryCarol R. Hunter, Brenda W. Gillespie, and Sophie Yu-Pu Chen, is a pleasant surprise:

"Our study shows that for the greatest payoff, in terms of efficiently lowering levels of the stress hormone cortisol, you should spend twenty to thirty minutes sitting or walking in a place that provides you with a sense of nature."

Just twenty to thirty minutes a day in nature to help us relax and rejuvenate our minds and our health. How can we possibly pass up such a worthwhile investment?

There's a decades-old Japanese practice called "shinrin-yoku," or "forest bathing," that consists of walking in, and being surrounded by, a forest. The idea is so simple: just walk relaxed in a natural green area to help you achieve calming, rejuvenating, and restoring benefits.

We can also invest in another health-giving practice called "earthing," which involves twenty to thirty minutes of taking off our shoes and walking barefoot in nature so that our feet can connect us to Earth's innate energy. The electrons given off by the Earth have extraordinary antioxidant effects that we can't absorb unless those electrons are in direct contact with our skin. They help balance our biological rhythms and energy centers. They're also a powerful anti-inflammatory, which means they can alleviate by as much as 80 percent the symptoms of inflammation-related disorders such as arthritis, chronic pain, muscle tension, and headaches. They can improve our sleep and blood circulation. They can accelerate the healing of sores, jet lag, and anxiety. The earth is waiting to provide all of this if we'll simply take off our shoes during our twenty- or thirty-minute daily dose of the "nature pill" and gratefully receive it.

Chapter Twelve

Brain Waves &
Why They Matter

Like many of you, I'm sure, I spent a lot of years believing that my mind was my commander in chief, boss, manager of my life. It had to be in constant control, ready to jump from one important issue to another to solve all my problems at once; always analyzing, always anticipating future situations and predicting their outcomes. I believed that worrying and anticipating equaled being alert, vigilant, responsible, and reliable.

From the time we're children, our families, schools, and society have a big influence on programming our conscious minds to worry, anticipate, analyze, and control as much as possible. This results in us also being programmed to experience stress, irritation, anxiety, and depression from the relentless mental pressure.

It starts as kids with our homework, grades, family dynamics, household chores, making friends, learning what we're good at, and learning what we're not good at. Then it moves into comparing ourselves to others, wondering whether or not we're popular, disrupting our hormones, luring us to drugs and alcohol, competing for college admission, and figuring out how to earn a living. Now, as if all that isn't enough to deal with, we have added complexities from the internet and social media.

We process an overwhelming amount of information from our childhoods using brains that aren't even fully developed until we're twenty-five. Furthermore, we do this without ever having been taught to give our conscious minds a healthy break, let alone how to put that processing in context with the rest of what goes on in our brains.

I was well into my hyper-conscious, hyper-in-control adulthood before years of hard lessons, study, and painful realizations finally started waking me up to some challenging questions. For example, if our conscious minds are really the ones in charge, why is there so much about our lives that we have no control over? We don't control when, where, and how we're born. We don't control who our families, classmates, and colleagues are. We don't control our external and internal life. We don't control the bodily functions that keep us alive. If we're in such control of our conscious thoughts, why are we unable to predict what we're going to be thinking a minute or two from now?

I was fascinated to discover how little I knew, and actually relieved to learn that I had less control over my thoughts than I believed I did. It was a very difficult habit to break, but I finally understood how much energy I was wasting with all my worrying and anticipating. I finally understood, and with good reason, that I could loosen my grip on everything around me without my life and the rest of the world plunging into chaos. So I let it go.

Letting go is important especially when you realize that our brains process thousands of gigabytes of information every second, making them the most powerful computers on earth. Yet, we are not fully aware of the information around us. According to studies, a person deliberately performs only about 3 percent of their actions per day. All other actions take place by rote from the moment we wake up, brush our teeth, shower, dress, drive to work, et cetera. And in the process, while we're going through all these automatic motions, we're missing life by being constantly engaged with our monkey minds. As a result, much of the beauty that happens around us gets drowned out by relentless debates going on in our heads. Our attention is consumed by our thoughts, most of which involve the past or future, while we miss the most important thing of all—our lives in the present. We miss the smell of the first autumn leaves, the warmth of the sun on our palms, and the starry sky. Sadly, we might not even notice the smiles of our loved ones.

We live and experience life's full potential when we're present in the moment. We can learn a lot about being aware and present in every moment by watching children at play. They're totally engaged in what they're doing, enjoying their "now" too much to be preoccupied.

Let's take a look at our brain activities in order to understand how reprogramming our minds can make us happier and healthier. Our brains consist of millions of nerve cells called neurons. They are in constant contact with each other through electrical signals. The electrical pulses sent by one group of neurons to another as they communicate information create brain waves that are measured in a variety of ways, including by thoughts per minute; i.e., the more rapid the brain activity, the higher the number of thoughts per minute. And we produce a variety of brain waves depending on what we're doing at any given moment.

Brain waves are incredibly powerful. They can form overwhelming obstacles and heartaches for us, or lead us to our greatest destinies and highest consciousness. That's why they matter, and that's why we need to learn how they work and how we can program them.

Our conscious minds, those constantly busy bosses we pretend are in charge, produce beta waves at a rate of around sixty thoughts per minute. Beta waves occur when our monkey minds are operating at full capacity and wide awake. When we're perpetually anticipating, taking in a constant barrage of information, analyzing, grading, and judging ourselves and the world around us. We can't find a creative solution to our problems when we're in this state of mind because we keep playing and replaying the same problems in our minds like a broken record.

Other categories of brain waves are at different levels of our subconscious minds. In a way, they're the real "engines" that propel our lives. Alpha waves, the gateway to the subconscious, occur as our brains begin to slow down. We naturally move through the alpha state twice a day—as we go to sleep and as we wake up. Averaging about thirty thoughts per minute, which is half the speed of beta waves, alpha waves are ideal for visualizing and setting goals. New research suggests that alpha waves also play a major role in the creative process, so if you're struggling with finding alternative solutions to a problem, it's effective to take a couple of minutes for deep breathing to switch your brain from beta waves to alpha waves.

Theta waves are our meditative, intuitive brain waves, and occur as we store accessible memories and emotions. We average about fifteen thoughts per minute when we're in the theta state of mind. Until a child is about eight years of age, their brain frequency patterns are predominantly theta waves, which means that everything that happened from before they were born through the first eight years of their current lifetime goes directly into their subconscious, circumventing their conscious mind. The brain is processing data, but the critical mind hasn't developed yet. The programming that takes place in those initial eight years will predominantly dictate that child's subconscious beliefs throughout their adult life. For example, a child who is continuously told that their only hope of being a successful adult is to excel in school may be programmed to believe that they're either incapable or undeserving of success if their grades aren't exceptional.

Delta waves, which produce about ten thoughts per minute, occur in the unconscious state during deep sleep. They're healing and recuperative, and provide us with a detached awareness of what has gone on and what is going on around us.

The delta brain waves also have a tremendous influence over the conscious mind, more than we often realize. The subconscious mind also responds based on images that trigger the autonomic nervous system.

Lastly, there are gamma waves, which create a state of super-consciousness where the brain is at its most awake and most elevated, with all of its focus on our inner development and Highest Selves. They're commonly considered to be the brain wave state of true spiritual masters.

A recent experiment conducted by science journalist Daniel Goleman and neuroscientist Dr. Richard Davidson unearthed some fascinating developments in our understanding of gamma waves and their influence on our minds. Their experiment took place in Davidson's large lab at the University of Wisconsin, a lab equipped with dedicated brain scanners and around a hundred employees. He flew in several meditation masters from Nepal, India, and France and conducted state-of-the-art tests by putting them through a protocol in his brain scanners. He was stunned to discover that the brain waves of these spiritual masters really are very different from ours.

Gamma waves are the strongest waves in the spectrum of the electroencephalogram (EEG), the test used to evaluate the brain's electrical activity. Most of us experience them in very brief bursts that last for about half a second. For example, when a solution to a problem we've been struggling with suddenly occurs to us, or when we imagine biting into a slice of lemon and experience a sour taste in our mouths. The incredible experiment in Davidson's lab, however, shows that for these spiritual masters who have devoted tens of thousands of hours to meditation, their gamma state of mind isn't just a split-second phenomenon, or one that occurs only while meditating. Instead, it's a constant presence no matter what they're doing. It's a part of their everyday life. Another unprecedented finding is that when these highly advanced meditators were asked to do a meditation on compassion, their levels of gamma jumped almost instantaneously by nearly 800 percent.

In other words, it's a logical conclusion that this gamma state of mind achieved by mastering the art of meditation is exactly what's been described in meditation literature for thousands of years—enlightenment, freedom, spaciousness, hyper-awareness, profound peace, happiness, is not just a state of mind, but a state of *being*. This amazing experiment proved once and for all that it really is possible to develop an elevated quality of mind that would allow us to perceive our lives and the world around us with happiness and loving compassion, while disallowing any space for destructive emotions and stress.

As an experiment, try to let your mind recall some traumatic incident from your past so that your subconscious will pick up on the imagery and alert your autonomic nervous system. Suddenly, you'll experience an accelerated heart rate, shortness of breath, sweating, and other physical symptoms of anxiety, even though you consciously know that the trauma you're recalling is in the past and not happening in the present.

This is a simple way to demonstrate a basic truth: Our brains don't distinguish between thoughts and real events. They react as surely and as strongly to memories and perceptions from both this lifetime and past lives as they do to what's tangibly right in front of us. Which means, among many other things, that all the worrying and analyzing and anticipating that keeps our conscious minds in chaotic, random, beta-wave anxiety isn't just counterproductive, it's invariably affected, for better or worse, by the volumes of information stored in our powerful subconscious minds to create a perpetual cycle. Conscious thoughts trigger subconscious reactions which trigger autonomic physical reactions which trigger conscious thoughts. So much for our conscious minds being the commanders of our lives.

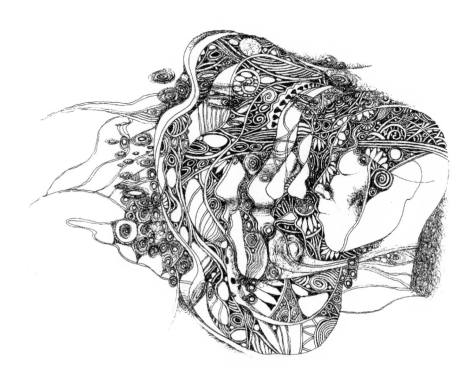

Learning that my conscious thoughts aren't as objective, reliable, and valid as I'd always assumed they were, and that instead they're heavily influenced by the countless imprints of the brain waves of my subconscious and unconscious minds, made me reevaluate my relationship with them. It was hard to do, but after a lifetime of identifying with my thoughts, giving them credibility, and letting them take up space in my consciousness, I learned to just observe them. I began putting space between my thoughts and myself and treating them as guests rather than as entitled, uninvited residents. I found that when I put distance between me and my thoughts, I opened space for my own peace and freedom. Rather than identifying with them, I let them appear.

I discovered that once I adopted the role of observer, negative thoughts had no influence over me anymore. The daily practice I still use to attain this state of mind is an easy one.

I quietly analyze myself and ask how I feel about different things in my life or things that are scheduled for that day, month, or year. When I find myself experiencing negative feelings—anger, resentment, frustration, self-doubt, disappointment, sadness—I stop and remind myself that they're just my emotions triggered by my thoughts. I'm only noticing them and observing them, even though my body's shortened breath and accelerated heartbeat are responding as if they're real.

I also ask myself, without criticism, "How long are you going to tolerate this feeling? Are you going to allow it to take over your day?" As soon as I start separating myself from my emotions and start seeing them as an experience, not as a part of me, a shift happens that immediately switches me from being stuck in the middle of an unpleasant movie to simply watching it, knowing that I can turn it off any time I want and focus on something more positive and productive. I realize that living in the endless loop of my own thoughts and emotions doesn't give me a chance to see the real picture. Life feels doomed when I attach the filters of my worries, disappointments, and frustrations. But I feel good when I see they are only a chain reaction and I can navigate through them.

The more I've practiced this self-analyzing exercise, the more adept I've become at shifting from participant to observer, and the less vulnerable

I've become to letting negative thoughts and emotions determine what kind of day I'm going to have, what kind of mood I'm going to be in, and how low my vibrations are going to go.

It's hard to describe how liberating it is to observe my thoughts and emotions rather than experience them. Those with regrets about the past or worries about the future no longer have the same impact they once did, and are no longer able to rob me of my happiness. The space all that wasted mental energy once occupied in my mind is now opened up so that I finally have a quiet place for my Self.

As the experiment in Davidson's lab clearly shows, our thoughts aren't limited by our physical bodies. In fact, brain waves can be measured by EEGs no matter what mode we're in, whether we're wide awake and active, sleeping, or meditating. Our brain waves create a field around us, a perceptible energy we give off, a mental body. Stressful, imbalanced brain activity not only damages the mental body, it can also cause illnesses that eventually appear in the physical body.

In order to balance and activate the energy center of our mental body, our upper Sun in the middle of our forehead, we have to learn to reprogram the mind's negative tendencies.

Chapter Thirteen

Neuroplasticity &
Good Mental Habits

As my curiosity about the brain and how it works continued to grow, I came across a *Huffington Post* interview dated January 19, 2017. I found it particularly interesting, and discovered it to be absolutely true. The interview was with Muireann Irish, associate professor at The University of Sydney School of Psychology, Brain and Mind Centre. She points out the significance of constantly challenging ourselves by learning new things and acquiring new sets of skills. Even though it's biologically an organ, the brain, like our muscles, enjoys a good workout.

"Recent research has shown," she explains, "that engaging in an activity that is unfamiliar and mentally challenging may provide the necessary stimulation to bring about improvements in a number of high-level cognitive processes such as attention and working memory."

Our brains are often compared to high-powered computers. And just as computer software is updated, the brain receives frequent "software updates" too. But neuroscientists have discovered that it can also receive hardware updates throughout our lives that continually form new neural pathways and connections. The brain can reorganize itself and change its response patterns in exactly the same way we either build or lose muscle; it can strengthen by frequent, regular use, and weaken by infrequent and irregular use. The process of our brains' muscle-building is called "neuroplasticity," not meaning to imply that our brains are made of plastic, but rather to describe how pliable and adaptable they are.

The easiest way to create a significant change in your brain is to invest your energy in a new experience. New experiences cause neurons, the brain's nerve cells, to fire. Repeating the new experience causes the nerve cells to keep firing. Repetition over time strengthens the connections and communications within the neural circuitry. With enough repetition, we can create new neurocircuitry to rewire and build new neurons and eventually cause the old neurocircuitry to weaken so much that it disappears.

Let's say you're struggling to recover from a past trauma. No matter how hard you try to push it away, you keep replaying it over and over again in your mind. Sadly, this only reinforces the impact of the trauma and even triggers the body to keep responding to it, so that it becomes more and more entrenched. Fortunately, it's possible to overcome this very common struggle by building a whole new neurocircuitry, with the help of new experiences.

My recommendation is to make a habit of devoting fifty minutes a day to activities that stretch and strengthen your learning skills. It will make a huge difference, both short-term and long-term, in the health of your brain and body.

When you challenge yourself to explore things that interest you, that's not about judging whether or not you're good at it. That's just about doing it. Enjoying it. Giving yourself and your conscious mind the satisfaction of accomplishing something productive, and rewiring your neurocircuitry to break old negative habits standing between you and the happy, peaceful life you're meant to be living.

Learn a new language. Learn to garden, or sew, or play a musical instrument. Take a class in dance, art, cooking, martial arts, or yoga. Volunteer at a nursing home, preschool, animal shelter, food bank, or with Habitat for Humanity. Sign up to help disabled veterans or answer phones at a suicide prevention hotline. There are endless opportunities to stimulate your brain and give it more productive, gratifying things to do than worry, anticipate, analyze, and replay past regrets and fears about the future over and over. Been there, done that, time to move on.

But if you really want to do something that will change the course of your life and bring you peace and tranquility, learn to meditate as a way to manage your thoughts and program your brain waves every single day.

Chapter Fourteen

Meditation for Brain Fitness

Meditation is a way to transform your mind. The practice develops concentration, clarity, and emotional positivity. It helps us clearly see the true nature of things without the veil of a foggy mind. With regular practice, you can deepen a profoundly peaceful state of mind. It's a transcendent practice that, with time and effort, will lead you to a new understanding of who you are and to the meaning of life itself. It extinguishes fears, anxieties, and other toxic emotions. I see meditation as my connection with the Source inside myself that gives me the power to live my life with grace and appreciation.

The formula: healthy food + physical exercise = healthy body is well known. The same formula works for mental health too, because our minds depend on the information we consume plus our cognitive capacity to learn and focus. But without exercise, the physical body gets weaker, and the same goes for the mind. Also, as we chalk up experiences over the years, unless we train our mental faculties appropriately, we find it harder to keep our spirits up.

The brain needs our special attention in large part because we live what we spend most of our time thinking about. Since we tend to become prisoners of our own negative mindsets, we become trapped in negative patterns with our own thoughts that turn into destructive forces against our own well-being.

Nowadays, many psychologists recommend meditation along with prescriptions such as antidepressants. Western medicines tend to heal not the root of illness, but rather their bodily manifestations. But unlike many medications, meditation has no negative side effects, and when applied effectively, can heal causes, not just symptoms. As an ancient, time-tested technique for training the mind, meditation uses simple tools based on breath, sound, and visualization to focus attention on one point. Meditation is a fitness program for the brain. You can live without meditation, but would you be truly satisfied with the quality of your life? To answer this question, you have at least to try it.

Through meditation, the scattered mind heals and calms itself. Just as we build strong muscles with regular exercise, we build the ability to focus our minds with regular meditation. These techniques help us become masters of our minds and therefore masters of our lives.

According to neuroscientist, best-selling author, researcher, and international lecturer Dr. Joe Dispenza, the purpose of meditation is to get beyond the analytical functions that separate the conscious mind from the subconscious mind. Our conscious minds, our analytical functionings, are self-limiting and separate us from our suggestibility—the ability to accept, believe, and surrender to information. Meditation allows thoughts to pass through the analytical filter and into the subconscious where it can begin to make physical and biological changes in the autonomic nervous system.

To paraphrase one of Dispenza's examples of what those changes can mean, if your conscious mind keeps thinking, "I'm going to be successful," but you subconsciously believe, "I'm never going to amount to anything," your subconscious mind will sabotage your success until it's reprogrammed to embrace more positive thoughts.

Meditation, then, can be one of your most important and powerful tools.

From a practical day-to-day point of view, this kind of brain training can bring you peace and tranquility and help you choose what and when to think. From a spiritual point of view, it provides an opportunity to really get to know your Self, and to reconnect with your Source by experiencing your own True Nature.

Remember Scarlett O'Hara's philosophy in *Gone with the Wind:* "I'll think about it tomorrow." For most people, thinking about something only when they want to is almost unimaginable, but meditation can make it possible. Once you've mastered meditation, you'll have a skill to help you build your life more productively, with more actions that contribute to your efforts rather than more of those standing in your way. Step by step, you'll find yourself building a strong house made of positive thoughts, where there is no place for anxieties, negative feelings, or fears.

Yet, many people are discouraged from even trying meditation because they find it difficult to sit for very long in one position. Maybe too they've heard that in order to meditate, they'd have to stop thinking. An important tip for beginners is just to *start*. To address the first hesitation, set aside three minutes a day for your sessions, preferably at the same time every morning or evening. Find a place where you won't be distracted by external stimuli, sit in a position that's comfortable for you, and relax while trying to keep your back straight.

To address the second hesitation, it's a myth that meditation requires clearing your mind. It's like being told not to think about pink elephants for the next five minutes—you'll think about nothing *but* pink elephants upon being told not to. The conscious mind cannot sit idle. It needs to be constantly thinking. It needs a job. These are our monkey minds we're talking about. If you take a banana away from a monkey without giving it something else in return, you're going to have an out-of-control animal on your hands. In this case, to appease your monkey mind, the "something else" is a meditative focus on the breath to replace the banana.

Focus your full attention on how it feels when you breathe in calmly and deeply, when the air passes through your nose, into your lungs, and down into your diaphragm, and then how it feels when you let that breath out again. Ideally, the duration of your inhalation and exhalation is equal to each other, but that's something you can master later. For now, all you have to do is be comfortable and relaxed, but don't fall asleep, and for just three minutes teach yourself to be interested in the external and internal sensations of your breathing.

At first, your attention is likely to slip away. You might even have an interesting thought or two. But those are just tricks of the conscious mind, the monkey mind, wanting to control the situation because that's what it's accustomed to doing, and it always wants to do things its way. When that happens, don't resist. Just let those conscious thoughts be, let them float like clouds across the sky. Treat them as guests simply passing through and return your focus to your calm, rejuvenating breaths. As long as your attention is devoted to your breathing, you are meditating.

The Most important consideration though is consistency. After twenty-five days of repetition, your brain recognizes a familiar pattern, and every time after that you'll find it easier than the time before to focus on your breathing. You'll increase your power to navigate your thoughts, and most important, you'll start seeing the spaces or pauses between them. And that is the moment when your whole new quality of life begins. You'll no longer be a slave to your reactions, and you'll realize who you really are, fully present in every moment of your life.

You can meditate anywhere and anytime. There are as many varieties of this practice as there are people on the planet, so tailor your own meditation practice around simply breathing in and out. Be grateful. Be patient. Be committed. You're building a new skill, a new habit for your brain, and your neurocircuitry needs time to be reprogrammed. It's really worth it.

Chapter Fifteen

The Power of the Self-Healing Breath

Breathing is something we've been doing all our lives on automatic pilot, and on average, seventeen thousand to thirty-five thousand times per day as healthy adults. It's understandable that we give very little thought to it, but it's also unfortunate that we pay so little attention unless we contract some illness that interferes with our ability to breathe normally and naturally.

It's unfortunate because learned healthy breathing techniques can relieve our emotional and physical pain and restore inner balance. They can overcome depression and the way our bodies process negative thoughts. They can override our ego's vulnerability to the stress of negative emotions like anger, fear, jealousy, disappointment, and regrets. Stress itself has a detrimental effect on the parasympathetic nervous system that under healthier circumstances slows the heart rate, increases intestinal and glandular activity, and relaxes the sphincter muscles. But stress can be controlled by a tool given to us by Nature. It's absolutely free—you don't need to spend money on expensive equipment or medications. You already own it, it's always with you, and you only need to learn how to use it effectively. That tool is the power of conscious breathing.

Many of us live consumed by our thoughts. We take our bodies for granted and lose connection with them by constantly engaging with our monkey minds; minds that at any given moment can turn us upside down and throw us back in time to relive our regrets and disappointments or hurtle us into the future to knot up with worries and fears about "what ifs." Conscious breathing can transcend the monkey mind by directing our focus inward and giving our bodies a chance to balance themselves. Every conscious breath brings our attention to now, to this exact moment, the most important moment of our lives.

Breathing techniques have been practiced for thousands of years, from the Chinese holistic methods of Qigong to the Hindu discipline of Panayama. In addition to all the other benefits we've just discussed, these techniques also help us restore our *prana*, or *qi*, the invisible life force around us and in us that gets diminished by all the negativity we let in. The clarity of mind and relaxation of body that we yearn for every day are available to us right now by learning and practicing the simple, ancient skill of these breathing techniques.

Our bodies were designed for us to breathe deeply whenever we want. Yes, we were born knowing exactly how to breathe deeply, but most of us we forgot that knowledge as we grew up and daily life took over. The daily habit of deep breathing from the belly generates vast improvements in our overall health. It delivers fresh oxygen to cells. It slows the heartbeat. It lowers blood pressure. It relaxes the muscles. It cleanses the body by helping the lymphatic system eliminate toxins. It stimulates the release of endorphins, the hormones produced by the central nervous system and pituitary glands that provide pain relief and feelings of general wellness. It relieves stress effectively and naturally.

In addition, deep breathing has a calming, almost massaging effect on one of the most important nerves in the body, the vagus nerve. The vagus connects the brainstem to the rest of the body, extending all the way down to the lower abdomen. It's a two-way communication network sending body messages to the brain and brain messages to the body. It's in charge of the sympathetic nervous system that cues the release of our adrenaline and cortisol hormones when it senses we're in danger or when our conscious minds are stressed and anxious. It also triggers false fight-or-flight panic attacks, and oppositely, the parasympathetic nervous system whose function is to keep us calm. In other words, deep breathing has a huge influence on the vagus nerve.

Even more is that the most basic deep breathing exercises aren't just amazingly wonderful gifts for our bodies, they're also easy and pleasant. They're quick and can be done anywhere you have a few minutes of privacy. No equipment, special clothing, or trips to the gym needed.

Here's one of the easier breathing exercises:

1) Lay comfortably on your back on a flat surface. Bend your knees, use a pillow underneath them for support if you like.

2) Lay one hand on your chest and the other hand on your belly between your rib cage and navel.

3) Take a long, deep breath through your nose, slowly counting to five, aiming the air you take in toward the bottom of your belly. Remember that your "target" for this deep breath is your diaphragm, which is located below the lungs. The hand on your chest doesn't move, while the hand on your lower belly does rise.

4) Exhale through your pursed lips as if you are whistling to a slow count of five, letting the muscles in your abdomen tighten and deflate so that the hand on your lower belly lowers to its original position. Use that hand to push out the air.

5) Repeat seven to ten times for each session.

6) Take a moment when you've finished to pay attention to how much more relaxed your muscles and mind feel.

A second similar exercise can be done sitting up. It's called "the square" and is especially effective for helping you relax, clear your mind and balance your emotions right before you go into a situation that you're nervous about, such as a job interview, airplane flight, performance, test, doctor's appointment, or anything else that might prompt the vagus nerve to alert your brain that you're in danger. Here's all you do:

1) Take a long, deep breath through your nose from your diaphragm, counting to five as you inhale.

2) Hold that deep breath and count slowly from one to five.

3) Exhale just as slowly through your pursed lips, counting to five. Don't stop until you feel you've successfully emptied all the air from your lungs.

4) For helpful imagery during this exercise, visualize a square, each side of which represents a count of five, and work your way around the square with each breath:

   a) Deeply inhale to a count of five across the top of the square.
   b) Hold that breath to a count of five down one side of the square.
   c) Slowly exhale to a count of five across the bottom of the square.
   d) Hold for a count of five up the other side of the square.

5) Repeat a minimum of three times and keep on repeating up to ten times, imagining that your anxiety is being expelled from your body with every relieving exhale.

These two exercises alone just a time a few times a day can make a big difference in your stress levels and overall health. They help your vagus nerve send a message to your brain and throughout your body that, at least for those moments of deep breathing, all is well.

Chapter Sixteen

Do One Thing at a Time

"Where your attention goes, your energy flows."
— Unknown

The essential life force called energy or *chi* propels our lives, but it relies on our understanding of one of the most basic laws: to fully apply chi's power, we must learn to focus.

Our awareness is the most valuable currency we own. Where you direct it is where your energy flows. What's present in our awareness becomes our reality, which means we have to carefully choose where we focus our attention because we don't have control over all our thoughts and don't know what they will trigger.

People who focus on the negative aspects of their lives are often easily irritated since their reality is full of negative episodes. But instead of changing this pattern by switching their attention to something else, they keep their habit of replaying negative emotions again and again. There are those, for example, who have a habit of scrolling Instagram, spending their energy and engaging their mental and emotional resources in order to digest what is most of the time useless information about other people's lives. Others move through their days unaware of what's going on around them. They're so immersed in their own thoughts that they're practically oblivious to anything else, and even when you talk to them face to face, they still don't hear you.

While other people we typically think of as being successful have a better than average ability to maintain their focus, pay attention to their surroundings and engage with others. Focus is definitely a driving factor for success, and meditation and other practices can help you get better at it.

One way that has changed the quality of my life by being fully present and focused on what I'm doing has been giving up multitasking. Now that I've learned the importance of focus, I work more effectively. I've found new interests and hobbies, I spend more time with my family and kids, and I even have more time for myself.

Channeling my energy by learning to focus did not come easily to me—it's hard for any of us to change our habits, especially if they've become integral parts of our personality. For example, I used to believe I was highly skilled at focusing. I was a working mother of three, involved in a wide variety of social and public activities, and juggled a great number of commitments at the same time, every day of my life. If I had to respond to an important business matter when I was talking with my children, I'd listen to their stories and simultaneously text my colleagues. I thought that multitasking meant I had a talent for focusing on one thing after another after another without stopping, or for focusing on several things at once, and that I was using my time efficiently in the process.

That is until I finally came to realize I was doing exactly the opposite. Not only was my strength and energy drained away, but by trying to focus on everything at the same time my focus was diluted so nothing got my undivided attention, not even my children. I was taking from them something vitally important by not being fully present, and in the process, I was depriving myself of meaningful closeness to them as well.

It took a lot of self-examination and self-honesty, but I finally broke a bad habit. Now when I'm talking to one of my children and a phone call comes in that I have to take, I apologize to my child, explain that what we're talking about needs my full attention, and promise that as soon as I'm finished with the call, they'll have my full attention again. Then I make sure to keep that promise.

I can see from their reactions that this explanation makes a world of a difference to them. It's reassured them that they're valued, that what they have to say matters, and that I haven't just been sitting there thinking about a thousand other things while they talk but am really listening and really caring. Not only has it deepened my relationship with my children, but it has also influenced their relationships with other people. They've learned that it feels good to be the sole focus of someone's attention, no matter how briefly, so they give their full attention to others too. They've learned how much more quality there is in a conversation when fully engaged with the person they're talking to. They've learned the importance of maintaining eye contact during a conversation, so are conscientious about that as well. (Note: Avoid looking directly into someone's eyes if they're angry, aggressive, or addicted to negativity. Negativity can be harmful to your auric energy, and it can also be contagious.)

There's no doubt that receiving complete attention is important, and giving it matters every bit as much. But we need to learn how to give it more efficiently and selectively. We need to make sure our body, mind, and heart are aligned with the subject of our attention. Whether we're aware of it at the moment or not, our energy is sapped when our minds go in one direction and our hearts and bodies in another. Being attentive to our loved ones, friends, pets, colleagues, and even to the plants in our homes and gardens is the greatest gift we can give, and as a result, the greatest gift we can receive.

There's a wonderful ancient Zen practice that can help us train ourselves to focus our attention. This practice can be summed up in six short words: "Do one thing at a time."

When you're drinking a cup of tea, just drink a cup of tea. When you're taking a walk, just take a walk. When you're reading a book, just read a book. When you're talking to someone, just talk to them. When you're eating a meal, just eat a meal.

Ask yourself how long it's been since you did just one thing at a time. How long has it been since you allowed yourself to be fully engaged in the moment you're in and gave it your full attention? How long has it been since you drank a cup of tea without checking your email, or drove without reacting to a text alert? How long has it been since you took a walk and just focused on the sights and smells and people around you instead of filming it to post on social media? How long has it been since you sat with a friend and really listened, instead of thinking about the errands you need to run on your way home? How long has it been since you played with your children or pets, or worked in your garden, essentially missing out on your enjoyment, instead of being preoccupied with all the things you "should" be doing?

If whatever you're doing doesn't deserve your full attention, why are you doing it? You deserve the peace, mental stillness, and clarity from telling your monkey mind to leave you alone so you can be a hundred percent in the present moment. I had no idea those things were missing from my life until I finally had them in my life, and now I wouldn't give them up for anything.

"Do one thing at a time" is one of the most rewarding disciplines you can teach yourself when it comes to stress reduction and reconnecting with the world. Like a "one *day* at a time" discipline though, it can be harder than it sounds because it's contrary to the hyperactivity that our monkey minds tell us we should be living. To prove to yourself that you can do this, and that it's very much worth the effort, schedule every day in your calendar a "one thing at a time" activity. Writing it in your calendar is more effective than just adding it to an easily dismissed to-do list. Keep it simple. Write something like, "Just eat breakfast" or "Just garden" or "Just walk."

Whichever activity you choose for that day's exercise, remind yourself that even if the activity only takes five or ten minutes, your sole assignment is to be fully present and fully engaged in it. When you catch the usual avalanche of distracting thoughts trying to intrude, acknowledge them with a firm and dismissive "not now" and then shift a hundred percent of your focus back to the present moment. This moment, this activity, belongs to you, not to the noisy, chaotic monkey mind that's trying to ruin it.

For the duration of this exercise, pay attention to the smallest details, and take a break from judging, criticizing, or having any opinions at all. If you're taking a walk, for example, notice every tree without deciding whether or not it needs to be pruned, and every flower and creature and blade of grass with no other thought but this one: *Each living thing I see is animated by the same divine life force as I am. A life force that connects all to this amazing earth we've been given as our home for this lifetime.*

That tree, flower, blade of grass, creature, and we humans are all essential parts of the same creation, with energy to cherish and share. So, if the weather and landscape allow, take your walk barefoot. As we discussed in the "Modern Challenges" section, there are those who recommend going barefoot for twenty minutes a day as a way to reaffirm connection to earth and let its energy bring reinvigoration. But barefoot or not, look at all the peace and richness there is to be gained when you "just take a walk."

The same principles apply to any activity you choose for each day. Be fully present, fully aware, fully engaged, and fully grateful. Give a "not now" to any distracting thoughts that try to intrude, without judgments or opinions. It's just you and the moment you're in with your cup of tea, or your child, or your friend, or book you're reading, or song you're listening to. Before long, when your monkey mind tries to convince you that you don't have time to indulge in something so seemingly unproductive, your confident response will be that you don't have time *not* to.

Part Two

Conclusion

"There is nothing either good or bad, but thinking makes it so."
— William Shakespeare, Hamlet

Unlike your immortal Soul, your ever-present Higher Self, your brain, knows that it is mortal. It knows it will die someday, and that every minute of life brings this ending closer. It panics, worries, tries to show that it is very important. Our behavior and reactions to the world around us precisely reflect this subconscious fear until we put everything in its place.

We must remember that every thought is a vibration we create, and only we can direct each one of them. We must remember that our thoughts are not *us*, they're just our creations, and we are the ones giving them life and power. We can create thoughts that are friends, with whom it's comfortable to exist, and who will help us through difficult moments. Or we can create thoughts that are bullies, that will not give us passage, that will make us feel disappointed in ourselves. It is in our power to stop the negativity and stop experiencing this discomfort. It is in our power to feel the pleasure of our inner state.

As an example, compare yourself in a good mood to yourself when you're in a bad mood. When you're in a good mood, everything around you—circumstances, people, even animals—respond warmly to you, and you think, *oh, I'm so lucky today*. But when you're in a bad mood, your frequency is lower. Every step you take can lead to more troubles, and you think, *this was a bad day for me*. That's how you create your own reality with your thoughts.

Changing the pattern of your thoughts takes time and consistency. But the good news is you can do it. It's very possible that after a month, you'll feel lighter; in two months you'll have fewer fears and less anxiety; and in a year you'll be in a better place mentally and physically.

You can begin to make this important, transformative change by noticing the thoughts that bring you to an internal darkness. When you detect the negative thought that triggered your bad mood, drop it immediately. Don't let yourself indulge in it. Instead, redirect your attention to the present moment. Using all your senses, look around. Notice every detail of where you are. See. Listen. Smell. Touch. Be fully there, in that place, in that moment, and then transfer your attention from the outside inward and focus on your breathing.

Take a deep breath and follow it from the moment it enters your body. Notice as it passes through your nostrils cooling them before it travels down through your diaphragm and reaches your belly. Hold it for two seconds and then slowly release it.

Our thoughts can break free like powerful horses and carry us, their riders, on wild gallops in all directions until we rein them in and regain control. Breathing is a step toward that control. Very often, thoughts cling to each other and create whole chains that lead to nothing but anxiety and depression. It's important to break these chains and return "home" from those dark journeys, but for that you need to feel the center within yourself. Think of it as a line passing through the middle of your body, and imagine this is your "home." When you find that your thoughts have taken you somewhere else, somewhere that frightens you or makes you feel diminished, use your breath to bring you back "home" as much as you want or need to every single time, every single day.

This is especially helpful for those who've suffered traumatic situations because we have a tendency to rethink and re-experience the trauma over and over again. We give those situations strength and power by thinking about them. Remember, our brains are like plastic, in that they are malleable. If you insist on disempowering unpleasant memories by refusing to allow them into your "now," and instead empower healthier activities and thoughts, you can rid yourself of old traumas forever. To eliminate them as soon as you feel they're carrying you back to a hurtful place and starting to make you anxious, breathe deeply to immediately bring you "home" to your safe place. If you want, put your hands on your chest and connect with the beat of your heart, which can calm you even more.

As a result, your brain will build new neuron connections thanks to the stimulation of fresh challenges. Complex tasks keep the brain young and active, so make a habit of giving it interesting experiences that will keep it fully occupied in the present moment. For instance, take up painting, learn a musical instrument or a foreign language. Attend exhibitions and concerts. Travel to a place that's always intrigued you. Fill your life with new meaning and interests. Meditate.

Everything is in your hands!

PART 3

THE EMOTIONAL
ENERGY CENTER

"Love is a decision - not an emotion."
— Lao Yzu

The heart isn't just a physical organ. It exists on many levels. For instance, it's a doorway to our emotions and our divine presence. Our emotional energy center, also called the heart chakra, is associated with the natural element air; this center is the powerful core of love, compassion, joy, and healing in us. It makes us feel whole and interconnected with every living thing in the world.

Love, like air, is formless, invisible, and essential. It gently expands to fill whatever space it occupies to give life. It has no biases, and it doesn't withhold. It's only when our bodies are compromised somehow that our access to it is diminished.

If the heart energy center is obstructed, we decline at our deepest levels, both physically and emotionally. Our breath becomes shallow and labored. We feel depleted, separated from our joy and all the love in us and around us. Our negative emotions creep in, and we begin receiving and projecting guilt, resentment, jealousy, hatred, and other darkness. The world no longer feels like a safe, nurturing place; so we withdraw into a self-imposed exile, not realizing that our middle Inner Sun, our heart chakra, has fallen out of balance.

Yet, one of the many gifts we've been given is the ability to heal ourselves. There are a number of simple and effective ways to restore balance to your essential energy center. For example, to reconnect with your heart, ask yourself, *how long has it been since I paid any attention to it at all?* Weeks? Months? Maybe even years?

Now, every morning when you first wake up and get out of bed, start feeling your heart. Think about it. Try to sense it by focusing on a moment when you were loved and happy. Breathing is an important tool for balancing the work of your heart and emotions, so breathe into your heart. Then, throughout the day, when you're in your car, or walking, or waiting in line, repeat that same awareness, that same feeling of sending breath to a heart that's experienced love and happiness.

Once you're familiar with this sense, you can awaken and open your heart even wider by making a habit of another very effective practice:

Sit comfortably, back straight, and let your breathing become slow and calm. Then, place your dominant hand on the middle of your chest where the emotional Inner Sun is located, and for three minutes, rapidly tap your heart center with the tips of your fingers, varying the strength of the taps from firm to soft. During those same three minutes, try quietly playing music that makes you feel happy, peaceful, and joyful; and silently repeat positive affirmations such as, "My heart is open to love and to be loved," "I love and forgive myself and others," and "I am blessed, and I am grateful."

Stimulating and nurturing the powerful heart chakra every day has an enormous impact on our emotional and physical health. It's from the heart energy center that the heart, lungs, and thymus gland control our circulatory, respiratory, and immune systems. We can't afford to neglect it or take it for granted.

To emphasize the importance of our middle energy center, our heart chakra, I'd like to share a beautiful discussion of it that was written by composer, drummer, author, filmmaker, and educator Layne Redmond, and excerpted here from her book *Chakra Meditation:*

> Our heart beats approximately seventy-two times per minute, adding up to 100,000 beats every day. Five to twenty-five quarts of blood pulse over 60,000 miles of veins, arteries and capillaries every minute. A well-energized and balanced heart chakra has a profound influence on our overall health. It regulates our breathing, the beat of the heart and the circulation of blood. Within this center air, prana and blood unite and keep the body and mind purified and energized. The heart center continually replenishes our life force with its pranic source in the air.
>
> As the heart pumps it generates the strongest electromagnetic field produced by the body. This electromagnetic wave vibrates the 40 trillion cells in the body on an average of sixty to seventy times per minute. These frequencies of the heartbeats are 100-1000 times greater than the electromagnetic frequencies of our brain waves. These electromagnetic waves can be measured radiating up to four feet out from the body.

Researchers have found that when people touch or are in close proximity, a transfer of these electromagnetic waves produced by the heart occurs. Using electrocardiograms (ECGs) to measure cardiac energy and electroencephalograms (EEGs) to measure brain waves, an exchange of cardiac energy between participants was measured. The signal was strongest when people were in physical contact with each other, but it was still detectable when they were within eighteen inches of each other. It became undetectable when participants were separated by a distance of four feet, the average size of the heart's electromagnetic field.

This indicates that we are constantly exchanging heart energy with people, particularly when we shake hands or hug them. As the heart chakra is energized and purified, love, faith, devotion, inspiration and harmonious balance develop.

Through meditation practices we have the capacity to radiate this energy more widely and affect all those we come into contact with. As our heart center strengthens we can vibrationally bring other heart centers into entrainment with ours. (Redmond, 2010)

This indicates that many ancient religions had it right all along: If we're searching for the core of our consciousness, we might want to look to the heart, not the brain. Indeed, in many religious and philosophical teachings, the heart plays a treasured, essential role. Even thousands of years ago, ancient Egyptians believed that the heart, not the brain, was the seat of consciousness. In fact, in ancient Egyptian, the words "mind," "soul," "heart," and "ear" were all synonymous with consciousness.

The Chinese doctrine of Chi-Feng Shui energy has always called the heart the "Emperor of the Body," since the organs of the body can only be healthy through the harmony of a heart that radiates vibrations of goodness and love. They considered the heart to be our spiritual center and used the word *xin* to indicate both the heart and mind.

The core of the mystical Islamic belief and practice of Sufism is best described by Sufi teacher Hazrat Inayat Khan: "Sufism is the religion of the heart, the religion in which the most important thing is to seek God in the heart of humanity." Sufism centers around cultivating the heart, and through it, finding sanctity in all He created.

According to the Upanishads, part of the oldest scriptures of Hinduism, the Atman, our eternal transcendental self, lives in the innermost space of the heart and symbolizes the soul, the breath, and the air.

The ancient Indian text *The Bhagavad Gita*, an essential part of the Hindu tradition, considers the heart center to be the seat of our sacred self, "the still flame in a windless place."

In Christian artwork, Jesus Christ is often depicted with a brilliant red heart that shines from within him like an intense flame.

To this day, Tibetan Buddhists regard the heart to be the seat of the mind.

The age-old, sacred truth of the heart chakra, the middle Inner Sun, is that the heart, not the brain, is the true power source of our energy system. And there are no greater forces on earth than those that reside in the heart: love, compassion, integrity, forgiveness, loyalty, inspiration, hope, and healing. There are those who would argue that aggression, violence, and giant armies are more powerful than love. But if that is true, why haven't any one of them ever led to the soul-deep, lasting happiness that love can provide?

Every minute, with every heartbeat, our heart sends messages to our cells and speaks to the world through the magnetic field that emanates from its core. Every minute, we create a heart language for ourselves and for the world we communicate with. Our hearts are like powerful Wi-Fi signals sending out messages and influencing everyone around us through our vibrations, with its magnetic field changing those vibrations according to our emotions. Just as we've felt anger, fear, or aggression, and love, joy, or peace from another person with no cues from our five physical senses, if we attune ourselves and our heart to radiate high vibrations, unconditional love, compassion, and gratitude, we can make a beautiful, positive difference in the lives of people around us without even saying a word to them. By focusing on the heart and seeing the world from the depths of this intimate place, we can also feel the fullness of our existence.

In each of our hearts rests a sacred space of divine knowledge, a space not touched by the problems and cruelty of this world. There is no bitterness, no grievances about the past. In this hidden space where the entrance and exit are open, each of us is in unity with God. While giving rise to, and an end to, our physical existence, it remains infinite. It makes us One, united by our true nature. Eternal. Without beginning or ending. Never to be born and never to die. Changeless. Timeless. Still. Pure. Luminous. Already and always fulfilled. It's only through this highest realization of our humanity, love, forgiveness, and compassion that we can dispel the illusion of separation.

Chapter Seventeen

Your Heart Intelligence Is More Powerful Than Your Brain Intelligence

"The distinguishing characteristic of humanity is the capacity to love."
— Rumi

What is it that makes us human and sets us apart from all other species on earth? Is it our ability to walk upright? Our ability to think? To conceptualize? To make tools? Do any of these qualities really lie at the core of our uniqueness? No.

Our ability to love and to have compassion does. We're all capable of giving and receiving those gifts, we just have to make a daily practice of it. A beautiful quote from the Dalai Lama expresses this perfectly:

> Ultimately, the reason why love and compassion bring us the greatest happiness is simply that our nature cherishes them above all else. The need for love lies at the very foundation of human existence. It results from the profound interdependence we all share with one another. However capable and skillful an individual may be, left alone he or she will not survive. However

vigorous and independent one may feel during the most pros-
perous periods of life, when one is sick or very young or very
old, one must depend on the support of others.

If we're not paying attention, if the chaos of our busy schedules and monkey
minds gets too noisy, then we squander the natural, precious gifts of love
and compassion. We fall into the trap of focusing more on our desire to receive than on our innate desire to give. We withhold kindness as if we've
only been given a limited amount and are not about to waste it on people
who "don't matter." We build artificial barriers around our hearts to protect
ourselves from being betrayed or insulted or disappointed again, when the
truth is that emotional openness and the ability to empathize with other
people are very much to our benefit and help us succeed in life.

As yet another example of science and spirituality becoming one, some fascinating studies have been done on the importance of *EQ*, or "emotional
quotient," as opposed to *IQ*, or "intelligence quotient." EQ is defined as the
ability to correctly identify and process our emotions and the emotions of
those around us. People with high EQs have clear, honest, and adaptable
self-awareness; they're cognizant of others' emotions and how to respond
to them with maturity; and they're secure enough to be able to applaud
rather than resent other people's successes.

In fact, according to an article called "7 Reasons Why Emotional Intelligence
Is One of the Fastest Growing Job Skills" by Harvey Deutschendorf, emotional intelligence will be one of the top ten employment skills in 2020. Few
schools currently have formal programs that concentrate on teaching and
developing emotional intelligence. There should be many, many more, especially since new research indicates that our hearts have much more
control over our brains than was previously thought.

Researchers at the world-renowned HeartMath Institute in Santa Cruz,
California wholeheartedly concur that the heart is intelligent and powerful, citing Aristotle's belief that the heart, not the brain, is the seat of
thought and reason.

One of the institute's founders, Rollin McCraty, PhD, observed, "The biggest hidden source of stress on the planet is the lack of alignment between

our deeper hearts' intuitive voice and our mental dialogue. This lack of alignment depletes the life force and happiness in humanity." He went on to say, "Living systems have the capacity to self-heal. Multiple studies show that heart-coherence-based, self-regulation practices lower blood pressure, improve hormonal balance, and provide better recovery from heart failure. Heart coherence facilitates better health and the body's natural regenerative processes."

Gregg Braden, best-selling author and internationally renowned pioneer in connecting science, spirituality, and human potential, points out that the Western cultural and educational emphasis is on the brain being the body's boss rather than the heart being the boss. But we can resolve the heart/mind split, or "incoherence," by creating new neural pathways in the brain through meditation. Meditation can help synchronize the neurology between the heart and the brain and ultimately achieve coherence. The HeartMath Institute advocates a loving kindness meditation to focus on the heart, activate compassion, and radiate that compassion to ourselves and to others. With about three days of practice, a whole new heart/brain connection can be established. Can you think of a more worthwhile way to spend an hour or so for the next three days to make a life-changing difference in yourself and the world around you?

Neither can I.

Chapter Eighteen

Be Your Best Friend

Practical Ways to Enhance Your Resilience

"Suffering comes and goes. Pleasure comes and goes.
This is the nature of life."
—Ancient proverb

Despite our difficult life experiences, we keep hoping, even expecting, that everything will be positive from now on. We make a tradition of greeting each other with best wishes on holidays and special occasions, and meaning it, as if we can wish away the fact that life has its own plans and always has two sides. The truth is, we live in a dual world in which we can't appreciate the brightness of a day without experiencing the darkness of the night.

No matter how hard we try to protect ourselves and do everything right, we'll never be able to avoid setbacks and disappointments. Every life is full of unpredictable challenges, regardless of how perfect it might look from the outside.

We're trained from the time we're schoolchildren to be goal oriented, to focus solely on results and success. We're expected to get good grades, graduate, get a job, get a promotion, and pursue status with all its trappings.

We're often afraid to venture outside our comfort zones for fear of failing. Wouldn't it be great if, while we were accumulating all that academic knowledge, we were also being taught how to deal with the self-criticism, anxiety, doubt, obstacles, misfortunes, and frustrations we're all destined to face? Wouldn't it be great if we learned to have as much compassion for ourselves as we would for a friend, rather than getting angry and impatient with ourselves for being affected so deeply?

A study published in the *Journal of Personality and Social Psychology* (Ford et al. 2017) made the fascinating discovery that, to quote senior author Iris Mauss, associate professor of psychology at UC Berkeley, "People who habitually accept their negative emotions experience fewer negative emotions, which adds up to better psychological health." In other words, we actually intensify our emotional distress when, on a bad day, we tell ourselves to cheer up and snap out of it, which, by the way, we would never say to a close friend when they're having a bad day.

Wearing a mask of positivity by suppressing our emotions can actually do us harm. We have to make room to express our genuine feelings without being afraid to face them. Rather than judging ourselves and scolding ourselves for feeling anxious, sad, resentful, or disappointed, it's much healthier and more compassionate to recognize that those feelings are normal. We've felt this way before, whether we thought it was justified or not, so we know from past experience that it's only temporary. It will pass, and the less we judge ourselves or try to avoid feeling what we're feeling, the more resilient we'll be. Remember that to resist is to contain, and to relax is to let go. As Rumi, a thirteenth-century theologian and Sufi mystic, profoundly observed, "The wound is the place where the light enters you."

Pain has the power to change us, the invaluable potential to bring us to another level. In moments of sorrow, when we're wandering through dark periods, we have to remember that everything has its beginning and its end. The darkness will pass, and the sunshine will brighten our lives again; we just have to be patient.

Acknowledging negative emotions, letting yourself feel them, and recognizing them as something you're experiencing allows you to create a space between you and what you're going through. You become an observer rather than a victim, a good friend who understands and accepts without dictating how you "should" or "shouldn't" be feeling. No exaggerating or overdramatizing, no self-pity, just seeing your situation for no more and no less than what it is, and letting yourself be imperfect, as any good friend would do.

Remember, you are not your emotions. You're just the one who experiences them. In our day-to-day lives, we can become distracted by, and absorbed in, our thoughts and feelings and often allow them to obscure our essence, the nature of who we truly are, in much the same way that clouds can obscure the sun on a cloudy day. Let the clouds pass, they need time to fulfill their purpose, too. The sun will always be there, just as your true nature will always be there, shining no matter what. You just have to be aware of your inner light, which gives life and warmth and energy to you and everything around you.

For those times when the clouds are still in the sky and you're experiencing moments of sorrow, give yourself a hug. Write the same compassionate letter to yourself that you'd write to a friend in your same situation. Comfort yourself, and notice how even your own soft, warm touch is calming and reassuring.

There's a hormone called oxytocin that's secreted by the pituitary gland and released when we make a significant social bond or just snuggle with a loved one, a pet, and even ourselves. It's sometimes known as the "love hormone." Tell yourself, with a hug, *I know it's a hard time, darling, but your heart is still full of love and kindness,* and trigger your own "love hormone" while riding out your negative emotions. Your pain won't vanish instantly, but it will begin to dissipate, especially when you keep reminding yourself that you've survived this darkness before and know it's only temporary.

And you don't have to feel alone and isolated. Remember, everyone suffers. Everyone faces challenges. That's how we grow. If you doubt that for a moment, ask yourself this question: *What have I learned when times were good?* I'll bet you learned less than when you look back at your "post-traumatic" times.

Perhaps most of all, you don't have to close your heart to protect yourself from feeling like this again. It's easy to think after negative experiences with other people, *I'll never trust anyone again*, or *I'll never help anyone again*, or *I'll never love again*. That anger, that impulse to shut yourself off and hide behind a wall is a form of punishing yourself for other people's mistakes. Don't ever close your heart. Doing that will isolate you and separate you from your Source. You can't let other people's negative behaviors determine *your* behavior, or let it affect your life, your character, and your opinion of yourself. How other people treat you is their karma. How you treat them in return is *your* karma.

Since energy can't flow where there are barriers and tensions, by blocking negative energy you also block the good, positive energy that's waiting to come in. Whereas a strong, pure heart is free from the weapons of hatred, the armor of past offenses and frustrations, and the sharp spikes of defenses against future shocks. It beats most proudly in the absence of fear, resentment, and bigotry. It's at its most open when it's unburdened from a refusal to forgive, because old grudges take up a huge amount of space and consume a huge amount of energy. The brain reacts equally to what is happening now and whatever we remember and imagine, which means that prolonged negative thoughts about someone or something causes the brain to cue the body to release stress hormones. It's a fact, then, that no one benefits more from our learning to forgive and letting go than we do. And since we can't give away what we don't have, it stands to reason that the more generous we are with compassion toward ourselves, the more compassion we'll have to give to all the other residents we share this planet with.

One of the hardest and most valuable lessons we can learn and embrace is that for better or for worse, everything is temporary. Impermanence is inevitable, it is as intrinsic to life as the air we breathe. This can seem like bad news on our best days and great news on our worst. But in the biggest possible picture, when we embrace the reality of impermanence and stop being blindsided by it, we can give ourselves the priceless gift of learning to let go. Letting go willingly, gracefully, and without resentment as a way of addressing our lives and the world around us leads to profound internal changes. It brings us peace, acceptance, gratitude, flexibility, and a significant decrease in anxiety and fear. Rather than being afraid of change, failure, and loss, mastering the art of letting go allows us to know that we'll be facing all those things sooner or later, and that they're impermanent, too. So whatever happens, we'll have the faith and strength to get through it.

There's a wonderful parable about impermanence that is very much worth sharing:

> The wealthy, powerful King Solomon decided one day to test and humble his most trusted minister, Benaiah Ben Yehoyada.
>
> "Benaiah," he said, "there is a certain ring that I want you to bring to me so that I can wear it for Sukkot, our celebration of the harvest and God's protection of His children when they left Egypt. That gives you six months to find it. This ring has magical powers. If a happy man looks at it, he becomes sad, and if a sad man looks at it, he becomes happy."
>
> Solomon knew he was sending Benaiah on an impossible mission since no such ring existed, but he felt his minister needed a lesson in humility.
>
> Benaiah looked far and wide for months for the magical ring, but without success. Finally, on the night before Sukkot, he found himself, anxious and dejected, walking through the poorest neighborhood in Jerusalem when he happened upon a jeweler who was setting out his wares on a threadbare carpet. He asked the jeweler if he'd ever heard of such a ring.
>
> The jeweler silently reached in his pocket, pulled out a plain gold ring and engraved something on it. Benaiah triumphantly returned to Solomon, just in time for Sukkot, to present him with the magical ring he'd asked for six months earlier.
>
> Amused, King Solomon took the ring and looked at the engraving. His smile disappeared as he read the words the jeweler had inscribed: *"gam zeh ya'avor,"* which translates to, "This too shall pass."
>
> And at that moment the king realized that all his wisdom, wealth and power were fleeting, for one day he would be nothing but dust.

Chapter Nineteen

Forgiveness, Hawaiian Style

In the middle of writing this book, I attended an herbal medicine class in Hawaii. That land of tremendous beauty, with its unique nature and powerful energy giving birth to the New Earth, has become an important teacher for me during my many visits there. On afternoon after a lecture, I went to my hotel room, picked up my laptop, and settled onto the balcony to record what I'd learned that day. Sunset played out before my eyes, a vanilla oil painting with a soft pink palette of colors. I watched it from the depths of my heart, feeling that the scenery and the colors were vibrations appearing in my consciousness and merging with my Self in perfect Unity, and started writing about an ancient, profound Hawaiian forgiveness practice called Ho'oponopono that's been changing and healing lives for many millennia.

Ho'oponopono's literal translation is "to put to right; to correct." But in the broader scheme of things, it's considered to be a pathway to forgiveness and reconciliation. Ho'oponopono is a practice that cleanses our minds and our spirits, with the power to cure the problems and illnesses of the physical world we all share. It's been refined by a Hawaiian psychologist named Dr. Ihaleakala Hew Len, whose method is called "Self I-Dentity Through Ho'oponopono," or SITH, with four simple steps in its core: "I'm sorry. Please forgive me. Thank you. I love you."

According to Hawaiian tradition, all life on earth is connected. A part of this belief that resonates with those who have different beliefs is the high regard for repentance, forgiveness, gratitude, and love: "I'm sorry, please forgive me, thank you, I love you." So the Ho'oponopono method can not only create inner peace and healing, it can ultimately promote global peace and healing as well.

Spoken silently or out loud as part of a daily routine, "I'm sorry, please forgive me, thank you, I love you" can have a remarkable internal calming effect over time; a simple way for both clearing and cleansing the mind, since everything happens to you in your mind. Whether or not you're thinking about the words as you're saying them, there will be days when you find them dredging up thoughts, feelings, and memories that are unsettling, even painful. You might get defensive and wonder what you have to be sorry for, or why you should be asking forgiveness. You might be feeling angry, or resentful, or unhappy, or in too dark a mood to think about things like love and gratitude.

But the same words that brought all this discord to the surface inside you can calm it as well if you'll just keep repeating them. "I'm sorry, please forgive me, thank you, I love you." The simple, responsible, harmonious concepts at the heart of Ho'oponopono, the concepts our souls and the soul of this earth are attuned to, the concepts that, expressed in words for you to keep repeating, can put you back in step with yourself and the world around you. Maybe best of all, they can help clear your mind.

The foundation of Hew Len's approach to Ho'oponopono is his belief that we all have the power to heal ourselves and others by taking responsibility for the conflicts we create and for the conflicts created "out there." The key is accepting the fact that we're each responsible for everything that enters our consciousness and how we process it, because, in his words, "you are in me and I am in you." There's a fundamental unity that connects us all, as relevant and powerful as our own personal reality. Cleansing, healing, forgiving, and loving the world around us starts with taking responsibility and working hard on cleansing, healing, forgiving, and loving ourselves. At least once a day, silently or out loud, alone or with other people, practicing Ho'oponopono can change your life and bring understanding that the "out there" really isn't "out there" because everything happens within you.

Chapter Twenty

Letting Go of Emotional Pain
A Personal Story

"Happiness can exist only in acceptance."
— George Orwell

You've already heard many times that it's to our detriment to hold on to hard feelings and resentment. Somehow, though, while we tend to accept that logic in our minds, we have trouble accepting it in our hearts.

People describe the effects of being insulted as feeling "heavy on my heart," or "my chest tightened," or "difficult for me to take in a full breath." Those reactions suggest that the pain that's just been aimed at us is something invisible to our eyes, something we can't touch, but we feel physically. Sometimes we experience a negative situation that we think we've put behind us, but we can find it rising to the surface again along with all the painful sensations flooding back with a full force equal to when the situation first happened.

It's no secret that many diseases, in particular cancer, can be traced to those same exact sensations. Any number of diseases are our body's reactions to aggression directed toward us. We ourselves create thoughts and emotions that exist as vibrations that constantly affect our energy fields. Furthermore, negative vibrations strengthen when we feed them our attention. They form energetic clusters of low vibrations that eventually pierce our energy shells and manifest as diseases. My own experience taught me how holding on to emotional pain can lead to very serious illnesses.

I'd always been an optimistic and cheerful person. Then, at twenty years old, for the first time in my life, my optimism seemed to disappear. I went through a period of deep despair and barely had enough strength to stand on my own two feet and face all the challenges life was throwing at me. Dark and difficult moments from earlier years had built up in me and had led me to immerse myself in thoughts of injustice and resentment toward myself, other people, and toward God. It wasn't as much of a depression as it was a pervasive anger. I directed it inward, and it took away my vital forces.

Compounding my bitterness was the fact that something had begun to dramatically impair my peripheral vision. In search of a solution, I went to see specialists in Moscow. The diagnosis was devastating. I was told that my vision was being impaired by a brain tumor that could cost me my life. At the same time, I found out that I was pregnant.

The news about my illness hardened my heart even more. It seemed completely unfair. I thought to myself, *I'm doing everything right, as any good person should. I never, ever abuse or insult anyone. I never refuse to help those in need. I'm responsible beyond my years. And my reward is a brain tumor? Really? What could I have possibly done to deserve the pain that has been directed at me?*

The question "why me?" was constantly pulsating in my head. There are people who do nothing but evil and seem to live long, happy, healthy lives. There are people who steal and lie, and who are mean, abusive, arrogant, and unkind every minute of every day but have no apparent bad consequences. Why me?

This all was occurring very early in my pregnancy, and the doctors were insisting that I terminate. But I absolutely refused. I was determined to do whatever it took to live and to give birth to a strong, healthy child; included in that "whatever it took" was finding answers to despair with the help of an outstanding spiritual master, who later became my teacher. Since my childhood, life has always sent me guidance through very special people and books. It's still true to this very day, and I feel blessed. What my teacher taught me, frankly, sounded simple yet soberingly cold. But this truth completely changed my perception and saved my life.

"Every person, every soul develops at its own pace," he said. "Some sit in a small chair in kindergarten. Some go to middle school. Some graduate from college. Everyone has their own assignments and their own challenges. What's important for the soul is to move on to its next stage of development. Sometimes the degradation of our soul presents itself in our lives because the soul's only objective is to grow. Therefore, for example, those who offended others yesterday, or stole, or lied, or cheated, and then realized that this is wrong and stopped doing it experience a huge advance in the development of their soul.

"Your soul has already learned those lessons, so you have another lesson to learn here: Stop getting offended and looking for places to lay blame. If you want to live, difficult, traumatic situations, pray, and meditate. There should be more love in your soul than anything else. Where love lives there is no space for insults and anger."

I listened to his advice and summoned my strength to accept it, follow it, and let it fill my heart with love, growing more and more confident that through so many difficulties, my unborn child and I would overcome this all.

The most important thing I learned was to forgive myself and others. I revisited all the major events in my life and fully accepted them. I realized that my strong feelings of judgment toward myself and others had the same quality as anger and aggression. I didn't want to poison myself anymore with such ugly feelings. Forgiveness freed me and let me see life for what it is: beautiful. And for the first time, I truly saw the new life growing inside me.

There were so many difficulties, but I still see those nine months as the most challenging yet inspiring time of my life. I came to believe without a doubt that the power of my faith and devotion can overcome anything. I never perceived life and people the same again, and I'm so grateful.

The birth of my first daughter was an absolute miracle to me and my family. When they laid her on my chest moments after she was born, she clearly, very consciously, looked right into my eyes. I looked back into hers and saw infinite love and gratitude in them, a silent, "Thanks, Mom, we did it." I knew then that I'd feel the warmth of that miraculous moment in my heart for the rest of my life.

Next came more tests and examinations in Burdenko Hospital in Moscow and lots of doctors guiding me and watching over me. They told me that yes, in their practice, miracles sometimes happen. I was given, or helped create, another one: no trace remained of my brain tumor, and to this day, more than twenty years later, I'm completely healthy.

From that indelible experience, I learned with absolute certainty that there is a direct connection between our attitude toward life and the moments we experience in it. I learned firsthand that our grievances and resentments don't help us in any way, but to the contrary, they destroy us by taking our life energy.

I believe that to forgive is not just to understand a person but to feel compassion for them. People who hurt us don't do it because we've done something to deserve it. They do it because they must have been injured, and since "misery loves company," they're trying to share their pain by hurting others. A happy person isn't motivated to do harm. That behavior is reserved for those who are experiencing heartache. We don't know what they're actually going through, but we can be sure they deserve our compassion.

In the end, the secret to keeping your heart open and not reacting to negativity is this simple: don't take anything personally.

Everyone's behavior, including ours, reflects our perception of reality. We each see and respond to reality in our own way, based on our own completely unique life experiences. No matter how empathetic we are, we can never really see the world through anyone's eyes but our own; so when someone is rude to you, or insulting, or aggressive, remember that this is their reaction to a history that has nothing to do with you. It might feel personal, but it's not. It's much more complex than that. You're not responsible for their actions and reactions, you're only responsible for your own. Don't let their behavior dictate yours. Simply pause, take a deep breath, and give time a chance to soften the potentially hurtful moment and put it into proper perspective.

Yes, you have a right to feel angry and frustrated. But let that go with a long, deep breath. Don't replay the situation in your head. Don't carry other people's garbage with you, and don't share it with others. You have the power to neutralize it with your intention and your breathing. Just focus on taking slow breaths for a couple of minutes and then notice how much lighter you feel. With conscious breathing, we can disconnect ourselves from the negativity around us.

Self-control is one of many qualities that distinguishes us from animals. If you have a dog, for example, you know it's instinctive for him to react when another dog barks. He doesn't have the ability to stop and wonder what the other dog is barking at or what the other dog's life has been like. He just reacts without deep thoughts and "does his job" of protecting his territory.

For us humans, though, who *do* have the ability to stop and think with an awareness that reactivity to personal grievances damages us at very fundamental levels. The vital energy of prana circulates through us along the main energy channel in the center of our bodies. If we're not mindful, our negative reactions to life's inevitable slights over time begin littering that channel until it's in danger of being blocked.

Imagine a clear, strong, sparkling river flowing free of any obstacles. This is the movement of prana through our body's energy channel when we're children. Now imagine that same river, its strength diminished and its course interrupted by a growing accumulation of pebbles. This is us as adults with a buildup of resentment, self-pity, anger, guilt, frustration, jealousy, thoughtlessness, et cetera.

Finally, imagine that river, us at middle age, straining to get past the huge boulders we've created that threaten to block our life force entirely and leave us dark and stagnant, unable to give and receive the vital pranic energy that gave us life to begin with. And then comes the moment when we physically experience that unpleasant sensation we talked about earlier, that tightness in the chest that tells us we've got some very personal spiritual work to do to clear our channel of all the self-destructive, unnecessary impediments we've put in its way.

We're all faced with challenges in our lives, many of them the result of other people's negativity. But we can't blame others for their life experiences and therefore their perceptions of us. It's their story, and in the end, we can't control anyone's behavior but our own.

The way to thrive in that reality is not to diminish ourselves by responding with negativity of our own, which strips us of our power and essentially makes us hostages in the situation. Instead, rise above it, refuse to let someone else's negativity penetrate our existence and become part of who we are. As writer Malachy McCourt put it, "Resentment is like taking poison and waiting for the other person to die."

There's a wonderful parable that has stayed with me over the years. I hope it will be as valuable to you as it is to me:

> One day, Buddha and his disciples were walking past a village in which people began mocking him and shouting insults at him, calling him a charlatan and a fraud.
>
> He heard them, stopped and calmly replied, "I do not respond to your anger. No one and nothing can influence me and manipulate me. My actions flow from my inner state, from my awareness. And I would like to ask you a question that might interest you."
>
> The people moved closer to hear his quiet, peaceful question more clearly.
>
> "In the previous village, people happily welcomed me with sweets, flowers, and fresh fruits. I thanked them but explained, 'I'm afraid we can't carry these gifts with us. Please keep them for yourselves, with my grateful blessing.' And now I ask you, what do you think they did with those gifts I could not accept?" One person from the crowd suggested, "They must have taken them home to their children and families."

Buddha replied, "I'm sure they did. And now I cannot accept your insults and curses. I return them to you to keep for yourselves. What will you do with them?"

Chapter Twenty One

The Health of Our Planet
A Reflection of the Health of Our Modern Society

It's gratifying that finally as a society we've slowly begun to realize and discuss our responsibility for the home in which we live. That home is our planet Earth. For thousands of years, humans lived in harmonious coexistence with nature, but somehow we've lost our way. We're robbing ourselves of this extraordinary gift by causing enormous damage that's almost impossible to repair.

We don't have much time! Due to our neglect and abuse, nature, with its complex wildlife of flora and fauna, might never return to her original sacred balance. This is our new reality, and the sooner we globally embrace it, the better equipped we'll be to take action and put a stop to the downward spiral.

In 2019, the Intergovernmental Science-Policy Platform on Biodiversity and Ecosystem Services (IPBES) released an exhaustive 1,500-page report. This detailed expert analysis was compiled from a review of around 15,000 scientific papers and government evaluations, with additional contributions from 310 authors from 50 countries. What the report revealed is an alarming wake-up call for all of us who care about our future and the future of generations to come:

- The average abundance of native plant and animal life in most major land habitats has fallen by a minimum of 20 percent, mainly during the past century.

- The human population has passed seven billion, causing changes to the natural world at a rate "unprecedented in human history," due to invasive activities such as fishing, mining, poaching, logging, and farming.

- Because of the very real phenomenon of global warming, wildlife is declining as the climate in which they evolved in order to survive continues to rapidly shift at a pace faster than they can keep up with. A growing number of plant and animal species, possibly as many as a million, are being pushed closer to extinction by a combination of climate changes and decades of poisoning, looting, vandalism, and other human violations of our forests, soils, oceans, and air.

- Every year, four hundred million tons of heavy metals, toxic sludge, and other waste materials are poured into our oceans and rivers.

- Plastic pollution has increased tenfold since 1980, and fertilizers contaminating coastal ecosystems have produced more than four hundred ocean "dead zones" with a combined area larger than that of the United Kingdom.

- Urban areas have more than doubled since 1992.

The speed at which this global biodiversity crisis is growing is a serious threat not only to our plant and animal life, but also to human health, prosperity, security, and even to the future of modern society. You can think of it this way. If we were to date the Earth as having existed for one year, then, relatively speaking, humans made their first appearance on the last day of that same year, fifteen minutes before the year ended. We've been on the planet a negligible amount of time, yet we've arrogantly declared it is "ours." Our same disunity and egoism has also led to us perceive our existence as being separate and segmental.

We don't perceive humanity as a holistic community, nor understand that we are part of a divinely created whole. We selfishly think that everything is here for our purpose, and that we have no reciprocal obligation. We only take and consume, often destroying everything around us in the process.

Yes, we are very far from an awareness of the integrity of the world, far from an awareness of the inherent potential integrity of humanity. For example, we ignore each other's pain. We kill each other. We doom each other to deprivation, motivated by dubious ideas. We monetize resources that don't belong to us, dividing our fellow inhabitants into the rich and the poor, the haves and the have nots. We're the only species on Earth that treats this planet and each other with such tragic disregard.

But we're too well educated about how living organisms function to keep denying the obvious: Climate change and other natural disasters are simply biological responses from Earth to humanity; i.e., a living organism's response to a parasitic invasion. Just as the body's anatomical reaction to viral attacks is fever, illness, and systemic disruption, our planet is lashing out with global warming and catastrophic meteorological anomalies to fight viruses endangering its life.

It's easy to oversimplify the ecological crisis by focusing all the blame on a single target, like the pollutants caused by industrial production exhaust. Though reducing carbon dioxide emissions is a step in the right direction, it's only a small step toward solving our critical environmental disaster. For that, we have to look inward.

We have to change our priorities and attitudes toward ourselves and each other, and toward every treasure we temporarily share during our lives here. Polluted oceans and deforestation are rendering vast expanses unin-habitable, and in the process killing animals to the point of endangering entire species. Is this how we want to express our gratitude for the unimaginably exquisite home we've been given? It's as if we're a bunch of out-of-control teenagers who've been left alone in a house and burn it down without a moment's thought to the consequences.

Despite our abuse of the planet in the relatively brief time we've been here, we're obliged to embrace an awareness that's essential to our salvation. We must understand this home we live in. We must dispel our ignorance and entitlement that's been exacerbated by having enclosed ourselves in steel and cement cities, and separated ourselves from life-giving resources that have supported all of our planet's creations for thousands of years. We are as interconnected with nature as nature is with us—when we try to separate ourselves, it is to our detriment and to hers.

"There is mounting evidence that contact with nature has significant positive impacts on mental health," according to Mardie Townsend, PhD, an honorary professor at the School of Health and Social Development at Deakin University in Australia, as quoted in a feature article published in *Psychiatry Advisor* (Rodriguez 2015). And according to Madhuleena Roy Chowdhury in *Positive Psychology*, "There are pieces of evidence that indicate strong environmental connections to be related to better performance, heightened concentration, and reduced chances of developing Attention Deficit Disorder" (Chowdhury 2020).

So do we just accept this information as the way it is and go on living the way we are? Or might it be time to change our behaviors and lifestyles? The answer lies partially in the government's annual mortality report that shows life expectancy in the United States fell in 2017 for the second time in three years. The average American could expect to live 78.6 years in 2017, down from 78.7 years in 2016, according to a report from the National Center for Health Statistics.

Data cites US suicide rates as being their highest since World War II, but due to the stigma surrounding suicide, it's suspected that suicides as a cause of death are generally underreported. The Centers for Disease Control and Prevention released a recent analysis stating that fourteen out of every one hundred thousand Americans died by suicide in 2017. That's a 33 percent increase since 1999, and the highest age-adjusted suicide rate recorded in the US since 1942.

All this suggests that, like our planet, people are also suffering tremendous damage. Yes, technologically we've made huge leaps forward over the past hundred years. But have we been able to make the same breakthroughs in developing our humanity?

People are experiencing tremendous stress, and judging by the growing numbers of suicide and chronic illnesses, we're not coping too well. Without the knowledge, tools, or coping skills to overcome our relentless stress, we're turning to unprecedented amounts of antidepressants and opioids.

What this means is that in a society focused on success at all costs, people are doomed to live lives compromised by depression and anxiety, with social networks ready, willing, and all too able to aggravate the situation. Consumption for the sake of consumption has become the norm. Clothing colored with cheap toxic chemicals is worn once to impress on social media with the hashtag #outfitoftheday, that boasts approximately 250 million posts, and then is returned to the store from which it came. A shocking 50 percent of those returned items are never restocked, they're simply shredded and thrown into a landfill.

Unfortunately, in the busyness of all this technological progress, we have failed to develop emotionally and spiritually. We're driven by our desires, conspicuous consumption, and instant gratification at the expense of our depth, insight, and clarity about the privilege and responsibility of seeing beyond our own noses and recognizing that we're part of a sacred whole. Instead of focusing on having what we want, it's time to start refocusing on wanting what we have.

This planet still has a wealth of beauty for us to experience and abundant natural resources to sustain us, just as a loving mother does for her child. But it seems to never be enough for us. We can't just take as much as we want, carelessly destroying what is around us in the process and depriving the earth of its ability to regenerate. Instead, we have to commit to self-healing from this consumption disease that compels us to feel entitled to take more than we need. We have to commit ourselves to taking as much as we need, but not one bite more.

Another tragic indication that something very wrong with our modern society is that tons of food are being thrown away every day while people with whom we share this planet are starving. The US Department of Agriculture estimates that more than twelve million children in the United States alone are living in "food insecure" homes. A 2018 report from the State of Food Security and Nutrition in the World delivers the sobering news that approximately 821 million people, or about one in every nine of us on the planet, are chronically hungry, and the number is growing.

These statistics sound even more heartbreaking when you consider the increasing amount of animal overkilling in our oceans and on our farms. A common practice called overfishing is causing catastrophic disruptions to the oceans' natural biologic food chain. Overfishing means removing targeted species from the sea at such a dramatic rate that those species are unable to reproduce and replenish themselves.

Large, aggressive commercial fleets with increasingly sophisticated technology for finding and harvesting their ocean prey are depleting whole populations of large fish; now those same fleets are having to reach deeper and deeper into the sea, and deeper and deeper into these species' natural balance, for their profits. "Fishing down," as it's called, is doing such alarming harm to ocean wildlife that the journal *Science* predicts the potential elimination of the world's fisheries by the year 2048 if overfishing isn't banned and ecological, biologic regulations aren't enacted and enforced.

While it's impossible to calculate the exact number of fish and shellfish in our oceans, we know that one hundred and fifty million tons of seafood were harvested for human consumption in 2016, with nearly half of it coming from trout, shrimp, and other aquacultural farms.

That same greedy, inhumane disregard applies to our dry land farm animals as well. *The Economist* reports that while the world population has doubled in the past fifty years, the amount of meat we eat has tripled. Which means if you combine the approximate total of chickens, cows, sheep, and pigs living at any given time, that number is three times greater than the number of people living on this planet.

This growing appetite for meat is taking a dramatic toll on our environment.

Approximately 10 to 12 percent of our greenhouse gas emissions are traceable to agriculture, almost three-quarters of which ties directly to poultry and dairy farming, with beef farming producing emissions that are four times higher than chicken or pork. But again, even bearing all this excess in mind, one in every nine people on earth right now is starving, barely surviving every single day.

I imagine your own survival doesn't mean to you a desperate search for food and water. Instead, we've all come to define our survival based on mental constructs about what will bring us happiness, creating a nonstop buy-and-buy race. We then implement this buy-and-buy culture in every possible aspect of our lives to the point where it's become our second nature. For example, during free time with our families on weekends and holidays, we more often go to shopping malls instead of parks. The catch-22, though, is we don't have as many choices of parks because we haven't planned for them. What we planned is easier access to stores filled with stuff we can buy even though we don't need it and often can't afford it, and fooled ourselves into believing that our overconsumption is fun. We mistakenly think that a new thing—a new phone, a new car, a new computer, a new wardrobe, a new house—will fill up our emptiness and make us happy.

In this endless, materialistic sprint from dusk to dawn in search of its illusory happiness, life passes us by. Even when we do manage to obtain those items on our "must-have" list, we quickly lose interest in them and discover that we're no happier than we were before. So then we turn to alcohol, drugs, antidepressants or other addictions, and destroy ourselves until eventually learning that the real happiness we're seeking can't be found there either.

In the march to fulfill of our desires, we've forgotten how to be happy unconditionally. We know it's possible. We experienced it as children. But somehow, we've lost track of our ability to experience joy and love and gratitude by just being who we are, by just existing on this planet with all its wonders.

What is the reason for our unhappiness? For our constant search for exterior fulfillment and validation? Is it that we understand nothing lasts forever? That we're mortal? That we're human beings? Think about what the word "beings" means. We're not human "work-ings," or "talk-ings," or "worry-ings."

"Existing" implies the main action of human life. "Being" reflects a life force, an essence, an animated vitality. We're human *beings*, impermanent and eternal; beings whose natural state is peace, born with an innate, infinite capacity for transformation, compassion, kindness and, at our core, love.

To realize this and fully embrace it is the key to healing ourselves and the planet. Love is our medicine. Our salvation. Our hope. Only love can save the world and us. Only love can soften the hearts of those in charge of others. Only love can make us see life's many gifts for what they really are. Love is more than just a feeling. It's a verb, a conscious choice. It's sometimes difficult to understand, but worth every bit of our best efforts. Only by fully embracing the restorative power of love and acting on it can we stop wasting our lives in pursuit of illusory happiness and start finding the joy that's already waiting for us within.

I wrote earlier that love must come from the depths of our hearts in order to illuminate our lives with the divine light of peace and awareness, and become like newly blossoming rosebuds that celebrate our existence. Each rosebud's aroma soon begins to sweeten the air of those closest to it, and as the bloom reaches fullness, it shares its beauty to give joy to others.

Love can, and will, cure us and our relationship with nature. It is a treasured gift to which we owe a debt we can never fully repay.

P.S.

I added this following paragraph in April 20, 2020 when the book was almost ready to be published. Today over three billion people, or half of the world's population, is in lockdown due to the rampaging COVID-19 pandemic.

While countries are debating who to blame, the virus has paralyzed life on whole continents and shut down the global economy. Every individual can feel its fierce hit. Even if the origin of the virus is manmade, it is still one of Earth's defense mechanisms to fend off our inability to see the connection between our deeds and their consequences. The virus is here to make us understand how fragile and imperfect the world we've built is. How our problems of enormous magnitude are fraying the social, economic, and cultural fabrics of many countries. And maybe to show us the failure of our system based on the consumption principal.

Hopefully it will make us slow down in our alleged "progress" and instead embrace a healing for the soul, a sense of humility, and finally admit that evolutionarily, the planet always wins. Earth has a profound intelligence and absolute resilience in terms of providing herself with everything needed, as well as providing for us as her children, not as her owners.

The virus can attack anyone without warning. It pays no heed to nationality, gender, or social standing. It is our common enemy, and this fact is helping us realize that people are the same the world over. One result is that COVID-19 has brought us closer in that we have begun to better understand each other's needs and worries. We have begun to better relate to other people's problems and to no longer say that our own troubles are more serious than anyone else's. A sense of compassion is probably the greatest lesson we can gain from this challenging time.

Conclusion
Your Limitless & Eternal Nature

"So we fix our eyes not on what is seen, but on what is unseen,
since what is seen is temporary, but what is unseen is eternal."
— 2 Corinthians 4:18

I don't claim originality when it comes to the philosophies described in this book, since all of the valuable thoughts I included have already been expressed throughout the centuries. Even if you don't believe in astrology, astronomy tells us that in addition to the visible arrows, the celestial bodies on the celestial clock, there is also an invisible arrow—the earth's axis. It takes this invisible arrow 25,786 years to circumnavigate the dial of the heavenly clock, the circle of the zodiac. In astrology, that completed circumnavigation measures the eras of civilizations as a whole. (The Earth's vernal equinox passes through each zodiac sign in 2,148 years, which means that each era lasts 2,148 years. Passing through all twelve signs of the zodiac takes 2,148 years times twelve, or 25,786 years.)

We happen to be living in a difficult time of global changes for the transition between two epochs, with the Piscean epoch having ended in 2013 and the Age of Aquarius beginning. The total change of eras takes about a hundred years and affects the development not only of each person's psyche but the collective psyche as well. Therefore, every zodiacal era must teach the soul something.

It was with the advent of Pisces, which can be described as the Era of Faith, when two of the world's largest religions appeared; Islam, and Christianity with Jesus's teachings to love one another, and to be saved by loving one's enemies.

The current dawning of Aquarius can be described as the Era of Knowledge, the era in which the practical benefit of spiritual knowledge will be confirmed by science. It will solve the challenge of optimizing the delicate balance between "I" and "We," the balance between the personal and the social. It's a challenge that requires spiritual growth, and it's very likely that in the Aquarian era, spiritual issues will become a dominant focus.

We already observe how science and spiritual knowledge complement each other by revealing a bigger picture for us. In the Age of Aquarius, though, what has seemed to be just spiritual knowledge will also become well known as publicly available facts. Science will confirm the correct behavioral ethics we struggled with in the previous era.

And in the not-too-distant future, we'll have a chance to become a better version of ourselves thanks to artificial intelligence (AI). Ben Goertzel, CEO and chief scientist at SingularityNET, a project dedicated to creating benevolent, decentralized artificial general intelligence, explains that with advanced technology and artificial intelligence, our global network will develop to the point where it will start making new Nobel Prize-level discoveries every five seconds and create whole new realities. With molecular nanotechnologies, we'll be able to build anything and everything out of molecules. 3D printers will be available to satisfy our everyday needs—from food to clothing to housing—allowing humanity to overcome hunger and poverty.

We'll be able to cure diseases and save lives by sending little bionano probes into the body to make repairs. We'll be able to reprogram our minds in a variety of ways, including getting rid of bad habits, being able to hyper-focus on subjects we want to learn about, and being attracted or not attracted to specific types of food, lifestyles, or people. We'll be able to redirect our perceptions of joy and abundance. We'll be able to fuse our individual brains into a superintelligent mind matrix and become one consciousness, quadrillions of times more intelligent than we are now. And we'll be able to lose our illusion of the individual self and free will.

It sounds like a whole new level for humanity, a total liberation from suffering and death, a time when we'll all be able to experience life as one consciousness, without war, hunger, and feelings of separateness.

This promising future looks very much like heavenly realms in which humanity in its entirety can experience peace and harmony. That is if we can get there before we destroy the planet and ourselves with some global crisis triggered by shortsighted, megalomaniacal, egocentric ideas.

With a worldwide understanding that changes are inevitable, and that we have to take action to survive as a species, schools will still continue to teach mathematics and physics, but they'll also begin, finally, to teach ethics, integrity, compassion, kindness, and other essentials that make up the core of a meaningful life. As a result of education being elevated, society will become elevated. This salvation will develop in early childhood from an innate understanding, and from learned knowledge right alongside children discovering the alphabet and multiplication tables. Future generations beyond that point will develop even more extraordinary skills that will allow them to truly know and maintain their natural inner state of peace, joy, and appreciation.

They'll be secure in knowing the truth of who they really are and in whatever role they decide to play in service to society. They'll do what they do best, without the pressure of debts, bills, and mortgages. They'll love what they do while benefiting society and themselves. They'll learn to effectively function on the many levels of their consciousness, and to manage their thoughts and emotions without confusing them with their pure souls. They'll witness all of their external and internal changes as being just appearances in their eternal consciousness. They'll know beyond all doubt that their true nature never changes or dies.

Their whole life experience will be refocused from the shallow external chasing of illusory happiness to the deep inner work of revealing and fully embracing the sacred, unique experience of wholeness. This knowledge about themselves will take away any confusion, frustration, and fear, and build on a foundation of love, compassion, and self-inquiry.

In order for humanity to develop harmoniously, it doesn't need hollow calculations borne of the mind. It needs wisdom borne of the heart. The source of this wisdom is knowledge. And only through knowledge can we gain the enlightenment to change the world for the better, a knowledge that comes from an affordable education and an accessible open internet without censorship. Or, stated more poetically, yesterday, you didn't know something, and that's who you were then. Today, you learned something, and it changed you into who you are now.

Far too often, ignorance is the foundation for intolerance and hate. So instead of increasing budgets for militaries and their weapons, we need to invest that money to fight against ignorance and illiteracy. The fortunes nations around the world spend on armaments keep growing, while we keep asking the question: Whom are we arming ourselves against? Those different from us? With constantly developing technologies creating more dangerous weapons, do we really want do go to war against each other? Do we really want to destroy ourselves and our planet?

I hope not. I believe the time will come when the knowledge we've been discussing will be spread widely in every direction through one-on-one interactions and broad communities, through personal art and international social media, through music, books, and movies.

But sadly, today it's rare to see an inspiring movie; to read uplifting news; to hear a song about inner peace; to find media that speaks to the strength of the human spirit or to the needed reassurances that everything will be fine. According to researchers, the most negative songs of recent years were the most popular. Evidently, our mass culture is a direct reflection of our moods and priorities. It's no wonder with so many nonstop messages like "I got drunk," "Gucci, Gucci," "I need a Percocet," "They hate me and I hate them back." All just human reactions to frustration, pain, insecurity, materialism, and injustice built by previous generations but still alive in our modern society.

We cannot underestimate the power of our current culture, nor the sounds we make when we communicate out loud about our places in this culture. We create vibrations with our voices. We create our reality with them, just as we do with our deeds, thoughts, and emotions.

Often, the reality we live in, the one that connects us all, is called a game. It's recognizable by scientific patterns and structures because it exists according to certain rules, and because those rules are designed to reach the ultimate goal. That goal is evolution.

Achieving it requires peeling back our ego to reveal our true nature, and then making a constant, determined effort to focus our inner energy on that true nature. Sometimes, being true to ourselves and making life choices based on that truth is the most difficult, painful work we can possibly do. In this context, our goal is better understood to mean "to be free," to be liberated from the worries and limitations of our body–mind consciousness, free

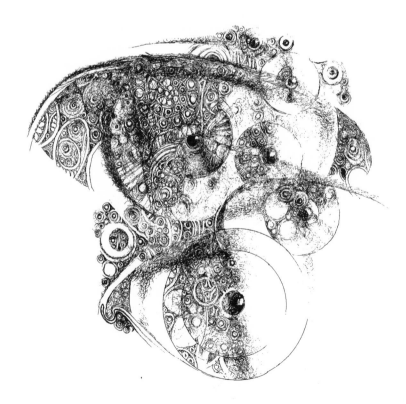

from our suffering and our fears. This can only be achieved by following the rules of the "game" by applying the moral laws that have been confirmed countless times by the world's greatest religions throughout time.

From the ancient traditions of Zoroastrianism to the Ten Commandments of the Old Testament, the laws of good versus evil are clear and simple. Yet, for many of us today, they often feel fictional, unrealistic, and subject to interpretation. Or we neglect them, which makes our lives rocky and invites unpleasant elements of karma (cause and effect) into our world. And all the while, we sit and wonder why so many bad things happen to us and look for someone else to lay the blame on. But as one timeless Indian proverb says, "We can't break the law. We can only break ourselves against it."

Throughout the history of humanity, the same truth about life and death has remained constant—that there is an inner presence of divine bliss in every human heart, and that our existence continues after physical death. Though this message continues, people often still seem to deny it and become more concerned with their external expression of rituals and feel they've lost their connection to this essence.

At the core of life on earth is the fact that we all share a common reality, and each of us by our very existence supports that reality. We're like waves in the ocean, inseparable from it and possessing all its qualities. Or, to use a technological analogy, we're like participants in a blockchain, a decentralized internet platform that supports and shares information and is automatically updated whenever a new block is added, like the ocean's waves, like our pure consciousness, both a part of the whole and the whole itself.

The existence that connects us all doesn't start with our birth and won't end with our death. It's not limited by our bodies, or by this reality we live in now. There is a bigger picture, an Ultimate Reality, that underlies our existence. When our bodies die, we'll perceive the reality we live in now to have been a dream. I know this as surely as I know the sun will rise tomorrow. I know this because of my own near-death experience. It is the most profound experience of my life, even to this day. It has changed my perception of how I see myself and see the world around me.

When it occurred, first I felt as if I had been awakened from a dream. And

I told myself that, *Yes it is true, I "quit the program."* That moment was more real for me than anything else I had experienced in my whole life. So what I'd experienced as my life felt more like a distant but vividly clear dream. We each have a special sensor in our brain that tells us how real an experience is. Thanks to this sensor, every morning when we get up, we're able to draw the line between a dream and our awake hours. The Ultimate Reality I experienced felt more real than the births of my children.

It's a beautiful thing to believe in the realm of the afterlife, but even more so to know of it from personal experience. That absolute knowledge is a blessing that has rooted me in the certainty that I am not my body, and that my life won't end with my body's death. I also know The Ultimate Reality perceives every atom of our world as a giver of life to everything, and that our world and our existence is not separate from it.

Though our life may be defined by time, place, beginning and end, and cause and effect, The Ultimate Reality is not, because it is infinite. In our world, time keeps flowing along, regardless of what is happening; everything starts and everything finishes, just like human life itself. The greatest thing about time is that it gives us the opportunity to see our actions and their consequences, from which we gain the great privilege to learn from those experiences.

Without this, human evolution would be impossible. Our bodies may not benefit from the passage of time, but our souls most certainly do, in part because a core quality of our lives is our own impermanence. Everything, including our bodies, is destined to change; which means that clinging to any objects we've come to possess only brings us suffering. Time, however, makes us humble and frees us from suffering. It teaches us that events occur as consequences of decisions or actions we've taken earlier, and these consequences will unfold over time through our limitless, eternal consciousness.

The truth is that our divine nature is ONE with The Ultimate Reality.

And because all our senses, memories, and actions unfold in our boundless consciousness, we unnecessarily limit ourselves when we define ourselves by our bodies, or the size of our bank accounts, or the status of our street address, or other mental constructs that include labels like "I'm a mother" or "I'm an American" or "I'm a scientist." Our true nature is too vast for that. It embraces the whole universe. To diminish ourselves with mundane labels is to weaken the greatest, most powerful part of ourselves—our divine eternity. It's a truth expressed perfectly and by my favorite Sufi mystic poet Rumi: "Stop acting so small. You are the Universe in ecstatic motion."

The Ultimate Reality isn't happening somewhere on another planet, or in another galaxy, it's happening in you and in each of us right here and right now. It and our existence are one. But even if we're not able to grasp this with our limited senses and constantly scattered minds, The Ultimate Reality is present in every moment of our lives. It is who we really are, even if it doesn't always seem to be the case, since our minds are programmed to keep us alive, to help us survive by calculating all possible threats in every moment. Therefore, its job is to confirm our sense of separateness from the whole. Our minds are fertile soil for overthinking and making destructive judgments toward ourselves and others. They commit to keeping us constantly busy with problems and worries so that we won't seize the opportunities we're given to transcend our self-imposed limits.

Our infinite beingness is primary. The whole material world borrows its existence from it. The world that we comprehend at the expense of our sensory organs unfolds in our consciousness. It existed before we were born, and will continue to exist after we die. It gives life to everything and is limited by nothing. It's an "is-ness" itself with no beginning and no end. By thinking of ourselves as nothing but the bodies we occupy, we deprive ourselves of remembering who we really are, of remembering ourselves through our infinite consciousness.

As the nineteenth century Indian mystic Swami Vivekananda said, "Each soul is potentially divine."

The negativity, judgments, and prejudices that divide us into separate nations, religions, political parties, social strata, and so forth are like filters covering the pure light emanating from ourselves and from each other. Only by lifting those filters, embracing the simple pure light, and seeing the same divine nature in each one of us can we start understanding more and stop going to war against each other. In order to reconnect, we have to seal out external noises, steel our minds, and focus our attention on the present moment.

By thinking of ourselves as infinite immortal beings, and erasing our limits and prejudices about ourselves and others, can we completely change our perceptions and, accordingly, change the world. If we want to change something, we first have to change our own attitude toward it. Only then can we positively influence our lives and the society we live in based on a global understanding of unity—meaning an understanding that whatever we do to anyone else and to this exquisite earth we call home, we also do to ourselves. I have hope that our planet and all who inhabit it will be kind, compassionate, and loving.

Notes

Preface

x.   Members of the Navajo Nation: Berger, Bethany. 2005. "Justice and the Outsider: Jurisdiction Over NonMembers in Tribal Legal Systems." *Faculty Articles and Papers*, January. https://opencommons.uconn.edu/law_papers/190.

xi.   Since ancient times: Hergenhahn, B. R. 2009. *An Introduction to the History of Psychology*. Wadsworth Publishing.

xii.   A few years later: https://www.lolakarimova.com/about-the-foundation, https://www.lolatill.com

xii.   From 2008 to 2018 I lived: https://en.unesco.org

xiii.   I was just a girl: Madiyev, Oybek. 2020. "Uzbekistan's International Relations," June. https://doi.org/10.4324/9780429327629.

xiv.   My destiny was: Akimov, Aleksandr V, and Gennadij D Kazakevič. 2020. *30 Years Since the Fall of the Berlin Wall : Turns and Twists in Economies, Politics, and Societies in the Post-Communist Countries*. Singapore Palgrave Macmillan.

Introduction

xviii.   Leading-edge scientists: Dosch, Hans Günter. 2008. *Beyond the Nanoworld: Quarks, Leptons, and Gauge Bosons*. Wellesley, Mass.: A K Peters.

xviii.   There is a belief: Blavatsky, Helena Petrovna, et al., Modifications of Consciousness. N.p.: Philaletheians UK, 2019.

xviii.   Pixels, by nature: Wissler, Virginia. 2012. *Illuminated Pixels: The Why, What, and How of Digital Lighting*. Cengage Learning.

xviii.   You see, every human: Deatsman, Colleen. 2006. *Energy For Life: Connect With the Source*. Woodbury, Minn.: Llewellyn Publications.

xix.   The foods and drinks: Klotsche, Charles. 1994. *Color Medicine: The Secrets of Color Vibrational Healing*. Sedona, AZ: Light Technology Pub.

xix.   Understanding neuroplasticity: Harris, Ryan. 2019. Neuroplasticity: *A Complete Guide to Neuroplasticity Techniques & Practices to Improve Your Brain Function, Develop New Ways of Thinking & Create New Approaches to Life & Relationships*. Kontakt Digital.

xix.   The subject of the soul: Bremmer, Jan. 1987. *The Early Greek Concept of the Soul*. Princeton, N.J.: Princeton University Press, C.

xx.   Each person's center: Peirce, Penney. 2011. *Frequency: The Power of Personal Vibration*. New York: Atria Books.

Author's Note

xxiv.   At some stage in its development: Fiske, John. 1902. *The Miscellaneous Writings of John Fiske*. Boston: Houghton Mifflin.

xxiv.   In 1935, Dr. Harold Burr: Morris, Joshua. 2013. *Acorns: Windows High-Tide Foghat: Volume III*. iUniverse. https://www.amazon.com/dp/B079J4TR8B/.

xxiv.   Further Yale research: Shumsky, Susan. 2013. *Power of Auras: Tap into Your Energy Field For Clarity, Peace of Mind, and Well-Being*. New Page Books.

xxiv.   According to Chinese cosmology: Wu, Zhongxian. 2011. *Chinese Shamanic Cosmic Orbit Qigong: Esoteric Talismans, Mantras, and Mudras in Healing and Inner Cultivation*. Singing Dragon.

xxv.   Albert Einstein observed: Seaward, Brian Luke. 2012. *Health of the Human Spirit: Spiritual Dimensions For Personal Health*. ones & Bartlett Publishers.

xxv.   Each level of an aura: Mclaren, Karla. 1998. *Your Aura & Your Chakras: The Owner's Manual*. Weiser Books.

xxvi.   Our three energy centers: Lefae, Phoenix. 2019. *What Is Remembered Lives: Developing Relationships With Deities, Ancestors & the Fae*. Woodbury, MN: Llewellyn Publications.

xxvi.   Our imbalanced abdominal energy: De Graaf, John, David Wann, and Thomas H Naylor. 2014. *Affluenza: How Overconsumption Is Killing Us--And How to Fight Back*. San Francisco: Berrett-Koehler Publishers.

xxvi.   Our mental Sun: Rutkowski, Anne-Françoise, and Carol S Saunders. 2018. *Emotional and Cognitive Overload: The Dark Side of Information Technology*. Routledge.

PART ONE: OUR PHYSICAL BODY & THE ABDOMINAL ENERGY CENTER

2.   The human body: Maitland, Jeffrey. 2016. *Embodied Being: The Philosophical Roots of Manual Therapy*. North Atlantic Books.
2.   In fact ancient yoga: Ely, John. 2000. *Yoga-Yajnavalkya*. Madras Ganesh & Co.
2.   Christian scriptures use: Version, New International. Holy Bible: N.I.V. New International Version. United Kingdom: Hodder & Stoughton, 2011.
2.   For example, our: Carter, Rita, Susan Aldridge, Martyn Page, and Steve Parker. 2014. *The Human Brain Book: An Illustrated Guide to Its Structure, Function, and Disorders*. New York: DK.
2.   The full discovery: Ewen, Robert B. 1998. Personality: *A Topical Approach: Theories, Research, Major Controversies, and Emerging Findings*. Mahwah N.J.: L. Erlbaum.
2.   The microbial cells: Knight, Rob, and Brendan Buhler. 2015. *Follow Your Gut: The Enormous Impact of Tiny Microbes*. New York: Simon & Schuster/TED.
3.   With the correct diet: Leitenbauer, Hubert. 2014. *Prana Energy-Therapy: A NON-CONTACT METHOD OF HEALING*. Freya. https://www.amazon.com/dp/B00RZMWYXC.
3.   New physics shows: Becker, Adam. 2018. What Is Real?: *The Unfinished Quest For the Meaning of Quantum Physics*. New York, Ny: Basic Books.
3.   We often hear: King, Vex. 2018. Good Vibes, Good Life: *How Self-Love Is the Key to Unlocking Your Greatness*. Carlsbad, California: Hay House.
5.   Just below the sternum: Myss, Caroline. 1997. *Anatomy of the Spirit: The Seven Stages of Power and Healing*. New York, New York: Harmony.
5.   All of which is instinctively: Gonzalez, Nicholas J. 2017. *Nutrition and the Autonomic Nervous System: The Scientific Foundations of the Gonzalez Protocol*. New York: New Spring Press.

Chapter 1: Life in Our Bodies

7.   The baby boomer: Paarlberg, Robert L. 2015. *The United States of Excess: Gluttony and the Dark Side of American Exceptionalism*. Oxford University Press.
8.   The diet of our: Kresser, Chris. 2014. *The Paleo Cure: Eat Right for Your Genes, Body Type, and Personal Health Needs -- Prevent and Reverse Disease, Lose Weight Effortlessly, and Look and Feel Better Than Ever*. New York: Little, Brown Spark.
9.   Our bodies are made up: Parker, Steve, and Robert M L Winston. 2007. *The Human Body Book*. New York: DK Publishing.
9.   Another life form: Foster, Kelli C. 2020. *The Probiotic Kitchen: More Than 100 Delectable, Natural, and Supplement-Free Probiotic Recipes - Also Includes Recipes For Prebiotic Foods*. Beverly, MA: Harvard Common Press.
10.   While medicine addresses: Rakel, David. 2012. *Integrative Medicine*. Philadelphia, PA: Saunders.
10.   But our gut: Gershon, Michael D. 1999. *The Second Brain: The Scientific Basis of Gut Instinct & a Groundbreaking New Understanding of Nervous Disorders of the Stomach & Intestine*. New York: Harpercollins Publishers.
11.   A balanced gut-brain connection: Mayer, Emeran A. 2018. *The Mind-Gut Connection: How the Hidden Conversation Within Our Bodies Impacts Our Mood, Our Choices, and Our Overall Health*. Harper Wave.

Chapter 2: Sweet Enemies, Chronic Inflammation & Fasting

13.   From the moment: Johnson, Rebecca L. 2012. *Your Digestive System*. Lerner Classroom.
14.   Chronic inflammation lies: Vasey, Christopher. 2014. *Natural Remedies For Inflammation*. Rochester, Vermont: Healing Arts Press.
14.   There is some evidence: Boyers, Lindsay. 2019. *Intermittent Fasting Basics: Your Guide to the Essentials of Intermittent Fasting--And How It Can Work For You!* New York: Adams Media.

16. But there are also "good fats": Gillespie, David. 2019. *The Good Fat Guide*. Sydney, N.S.W.: Pan Macmillan Australia.

16. None of this: Carr, Allen. 2016. *Good Sugar Bad Sugar: Eat Yourself Free from Sugar and Carb Addiction*. London: Arcturus.

16. In fact, Dr. Nicole Avena: Schulte, Erica M., Nicole M. Avena, and Ashley N. Gearhardt. 2015. "Which Foods May Be Addictive? The Roles of Processing, Fat Content, and Glycemic Load." Edited by Tiffany L. Weir. PLOS ONE 10 (2): e0117959. https://doi.org/10.1371/journal.pone.0117959.

Chapter 3: The Truth about Calories

19. In 1896 Wilbur Atwater: Spear, Susan E. 2017. *Mission Nutrition: Calories Matter But They Don't Count ... at Least Not the Way You Think They Do*. Gilbert, AZ: Nutrutious Insight.

20. This might work: Buettner, Dan. 2015. *The Blue Zones Solution: Eating and Living Like the World's Healthiest People*. Hanover, PA: National Geographic Society.

20. Not coincidentally: Engel, Jonathan. 2018. *Fat Nation: A History of Obesity in America*. Lanham, Maryland: Rowman & Littlefield.

20. But that didn't deter: Brown, Judith. 2016. *Nutrition Now*. Cengage Learning, Inc.

22. We've eaten our way: Sabaté, Joan. 2019. *Environmental Nutrition: Connecting Health and Nutrition with Environmentally Sustainable Diets*. Academic.

Chapter 4: The "Food" Industry

23. If it weren't for cooking: Shewfelt, Robert L. 2016. *In Defense of Processed Food: It's Not Nearly As Bad As You Think*. Copernicus Books.

23. By the 1980s: Temple, Nicola. 2018. *Best Before: The Evolution and Future of Processed Food*. Bloomsbury Sigma.

24. It's obscene that: Warner, Melanie. 2013. *Pandora's Lunchbox: How Processed Food Took Over the American Meal*. New York: Scribner Book Company.

Chapter 5: Vegan: To Be, or Not to Be

25. The question of whether humans: Ward, Peter D. 2015. *A New History of Life: The Radical New Discoveries About the Origins and Evolution of Life on Earth*. New York, NY: Bloomsbury Publishing.

26. The growth in meat consumption: Berson, Josh. 2019. *The Meat Question: Animals, Humans, and the Deep History of Food*. Random House.

27. My decision to become: Bramble, Ben, and Bob Fischer. 2016. *The Moral Complexities of Eating Meat*. New York, NY: Oxford University Press.

27. There's no question: Young, Rosamund. 2020. *The Secret Life of Cows*. Penguin Books.

27. The truth is: Ffrench, Rebecca. 2016. *Whole Protein Vegetarian: Delicious Plant-Based Recipes With Essential Amino Acids For Health and Well-Being*. Woodstock, VT: Countryman Press.

28. They discovered that cheese: Alisa Marie Fleming. 2018. *Go Dairy Free: The Ultimate Guide and Cookbook For Milk Allergies, Lactose Intolerance, and Casein-Free Living*. Dallas, TX: Benbella Books.

28. Among his many discoveries: Campbell, T. Colin. 2017. *The China Study : The Most Comprehensive Study of Nutrition Ever Conducted and the Startling Implications for Diet, Weight Loss and Long-Term Health*. Dallas, TX: Benbella Books, Inc.

Chapter 6: A Balanced Daily Diet & High-Frequency Food

46. Many people, after: Li, William W. 2019. *Eat to Beat Disease: The New Science of How Your Body Can Heal Itself*. New York: Grand Central Publishing.

46. It's imperative that: Openshaw, Robyn. 2017. *Vibe: Unlock the Energetic Frequencies of Limitless Health, Love & Success*. Gallery Books.

47. In an interview: Barber, Susan. 2000. "Bioenergy Fields: The End of All Disease? With Valerie Hunt." The Spirit of Ma'at. November 2000. http://www.spiritofmaat.com/archive/nov1/vh.htm.

48. In 1992, a plant geneticist: Shelton, Will. 2017. *Investing In Your Health... You'll Love the Returns.* First Edition Design Publishing.
48. There is a theory: Winters, Nasha, and Jess Higgins Kelley. 2017. *The Metabolic Approach to Cancer: Integrating Deep Nutrition, the Ketogenic Diet, and Nontoxic Bio-Individualized Therapies.* White River Junction, Vermont: Chelsea Green Publishing.
49. Further clinical research: Rodin, Kathleen. 2018. *Reboot: Release Emotions and Remember Wholeness Using Essential Oils.* Oily Baalievers Publishing.
50. For instance, chia seeds: Reinhard, Tonia. 2014. *Superfoods: The Healthiest Foods on the Planet.* Buffalo, NY: Firefly Books.
51. Many people also thrive: Waxman, Denny, and Susan Waxman. 2015. *The Complete Macrobiotic Diet.* New York: Pegasus Books.

Chapter 7: The Gluten-Free Diet Myth

53. In many cases, it: Levinovitz, Alan. 2015. *The Gluten Lie: And Other Myths About What You Eat.* New York: Regan Arts.
54. According to Harry Balzer: Yafa, Stephen H. 2015. *Grain of Truth: The Real Case for and against Wheat and Gluten.* New York, NY: Avery.
54. Yes there are adult-onset allergies: Esposito, Jennifer. 2014. *Jennifer's Way: My Journey With Celiac Disease--What Doctors Don't Tell You and How You Can Learn to Live Again.* Boston: Da Capo Lifelong Books.
55. Eliminate those breads: Bauer, Joy. 2018. *Joy's Simple Food Remedies: Tasty Cures For Whatever's Ailing You.* Carlsbad, California: Hay House, Inc.
55. Sugar and processed foods: Taubes, Gary. 2017. *The Case Against Sugar.* New York: Anchor Books.

Chapter 8: Life after I Quit Caffeine & Alcohol

58. People mistakenly believe: Stephen Snehan Cherniske. 2008. *Caffeine Blues Wake up to the Hidden Dangers of America's #1 Drug.* Boston: Grand Central Publishing.
58. Switching to decaffeinated: Carpenter, Murray. 2015. *Caffeinated: How Our Daily Habit Helps, Hurts, and Hooks Us.* New York: Plume Books.
59. Cacao, for example: Aster. 2018. *Cacao Cookbook: Discover the Health Benefits and Uses of Cacao, With 50 Delicious Recipes.* London: Aster.
60. Another great alternative: Gladstar, Rosemary. 2008. *Rosemary Gladstar's Herbal Recipes for Vibrant Health: 175 Teas, Tonics, Oils, Salves, Tinctures, and Other Natural Remedies For the Entire Family.* North Adams, MA: Storey Pub.
60. And in the bigger picture: Dry January. 2018. *Try Dry: The Official Guide to a Month Off Booze.* London: Square Peg.
61. It's a common misconception: Warrington, Ruby. 2019. *Sober Curious: The Blissful Sleep, Greater Focus, Limitless Presence, and Deep Connection Awaiting Us All on the Other Side of Alcohol.* New York, NY: Harperone.
62. Research also shows: Grace, Annie. 2018. *This Naked Mind: Control Alcohol, Find Freedom, Discover Happiness & Change Your Life.* New York: Avery.
62. In fact, the Global: Communication: Jernigan, David. 2017. "Global Developments in Alcohol Policies: Progress in Implementation of the WHO Global Strategy to Reduce the Harmful Use of Alcohol since 2010." https://www.who.int/substance_abuse/activities/fadab/msb_adab_gas_progress_report.pdf?ua=1.

Chapter 9: Better Sleep, Better Life: Deep Sleep, Its Benefits, & Tips on How to Achieve It

65. We also know how: Centers for Disease Control and Prevention. "Sleep and Sleep Disorders." Centers for Disease Control and Prevention. 2019. https://www.cdc.gov/sleep/index.html.
65. Our bodies and minds: Walker, Matthew. 2017. *Why We Sleep: Unlocking the Power of Sleep and Dream.* Scribner Book Company.
67. Deep sleep is undoubtedly: Thompson, Evan. 2015. *Waking, Dreaming, Being: Self and*

Consciousness in Neuroscience, Meditation, and Philosophy. New York: Columbia University Press.

67. According to cosmology: Perlov, Delia, and Alex Vilenkin. 2018. *Cosmology for the Curious.* Springer.

68. One of the world's: Muller, F. Max, translator., The Upanishads, Parts I and II. United States: Dover Publications, 2012.

68. Further, when we awaken: Thompson, Evan. 2015. *Waking, Dreaming, Being: Self and Consciousness in Neuroscience, Meditation, and Philosophy.* New York: Columbia University Press.

68. Another important aspect: Littlehales, Nick. 2018. *Sleep: The Myth of 8 Hours, the Power of Naps, and the New Plan to Recharge Your Body and Mind.* New York, NY: Da Capo Lifelong Books.

Chapter 10: Fascia & Yoga: New Importance for an Ancient Practice

71. If you've never heard: Muller, Divo, and Karin Hertzer. 2017. *Train Your Fascia Tone Your Body: The Successful Method to Form Firm Connective Tissue.* Meyer & Meyer Media.

72. Fascia consists of collagen: Larkam, Elizabeth J. 2017. *Fascia In Motion: Fascia-Focused Movement For Pilates.* Edinburgh: Handspring Publishing.

73. Yoga is one example: Avison, Joanne. 2015. *Yoga: Fascia, Form and Functional Movement.* Edinburgh: Handspring Publishing.

73. Tom Myers, author of: Gurtner, Karin, and Thomas W Myers. 2019. *Anatomy Trains in Motion: Embrain and Embody Myofascial Meridian Anatomy.* Independently Published.

74. Yoga practitioners call it: Lasater, Judith. 2015. *Living Your Yoga: Finding the Spiritual In Everyday Life.* Berkeley, California: Rodmell Press.

74. The fascinating truth: Skinner, Stephen. 2009. *Sacred Geometry: Deciphering the Code.* New York: Sterling.

Part One Conclusion

75. We can't ingest anything: Guo, Bisong, and Andrew Powell. 2001. *Listen to Your Body: The Wisdom of the Dao.* Honolulu: University Of Hawaii Press.

76. The ancient Chinese self-healing: Ni, Mao Shing. 2008. *Secrets of Self-Healing: Harness Nature's Power to Heal Common Ailments, Boost Your Vitality, and Achieve Optimum Wellness.* New York, NY: Avery.

76. The ancient Greek physician: Hippocrates, J Chadwick, G E R Lloyd, and W N Mann. 1984. *Hippocratic Writings.* Penguin.

76. We need to conduct: Bartholomew, Rachel, and Mandy Pearson. 2014. *Mindful Eating: Stop Mindless Eating and Learn to Nourish Body and Soul.* Cico.

PART TWO: THE MENTAL ENERGY CENTER

80. Experience doesn't just come: Romeo, Elisa. 2015. Meet Your Soul: *A Powerful Guide to Connect with Your Most Sacred Self.* Hay House.

80. Knowing that we have: Mcclelland, Norman C. 2010. *Encyclopedia of Reincarnation and Karma.* Mcfarland & Company.

80. I believe in reincarnation: Weiss, Brian L. 1988. *Many Lives, Many Masters: The True Story of a Prominent Psychiatrist, His Young Patient, and the Past-Life Therapy That Changed Both Their Lives.* New York: Touchstone Books.

81. Scientific opinion suggests that: New Scientist. 2017. *Your Conscious Mind: Unravelling the Greatest Mystery of the Human Brain.* Boston, MA: Nicholas Brealey Publishing.

Chapter 11: Modern Challenges

83. Today we live in: Stossel, Scott. 2015. *My Age of Anxiety: Fear, Hope, Dread, and the Search for Peace of Mind.* New York: Vintage.

84. For thousands of years: Ryan, Christopher. 2019. *Civilized to Death: The Price of Progress.* New York: Avid Reader Press.

85. A study called "Urban Nature: Hunter, MaryCarol R., Brenda W. Gillespie, and Sophie Yu-Pu Chen. 2019. "Urban Nature Experiences Reduce Stress in the Context of Daily Life Based on Salivary Biomarkers." *Frontiers in Psychology* 10 (April). https://doi.org/10.3389/fpsyg.2019.00722.

86. There's a decades-old: Li, Qing. 2018. *Forest Bathing: How Trees Can Help You Find Health and Happiness.* New York, NY: Viking.

86. We can also invest: Ober, Clinton. 2014. *Earthing: The Most Important Health Discovery Ever!* Basic Health Publications.

Chapter 12: Brain Waves & Why They Matter

87. From the time we're children: Hanson, Rick, and Richard Mendius. 2009. *Buddha's Brain: The Practical Neuroscience of Happiness, Love, and Wisdom.* Oakland, CA: New Harbinger Publications.

88. Letting go is important: Annibali, Joseph A. 2015. *Reclaim Your Brain: How to Calm Your Thoughts, Heal Your Mind, and Bring Your Life Back Under Control.* New York: Avery.

89. We live and experience life's: Tolle, Eckhart. 2004. *The Power of Now: A Guide to Spiritual Enlightenment.* New World Library.

90. Alpha waves, the gateway: Fields, R. Douglas. 2020. *Electric Brain: How the New Science of Brainwaves Reads Minds, Tells Us How We Learn, and Helps Us Change for the Better.* Dallas, TX: Benbella Books, Inc.

91. Their experiment took place: Goleman, Daniel, and Richard J Davidson. 2017. *Altered Traits: Science Reveals How Meditation Changes Your Mind, Brain, and Body.* Avery.

91. Gamma waves are the strongest: Goleman, Daniel, and Richard J Davidson. 2017. *Altered Traits: Science Reveals How Meditation Changes Your Mind, Brain, and Body.* Avery.

92. Conscious thoughts trigger subconscious: Siegel, Daniel J, and Marion Fried Solomon. 2020. *Mind, Consciousness, and Well-Being.* New York: W. W. Norton & Company.

93. I discovered that once: Kabat-Zinn, Jon. 2013. *Full Catastrophe Living: Using the Wisdom of Your Body and Mind to Face Stress, Pain, and Illness.* New York: Bantam Books.

Chapter 13: Neuroplasticity & Good Mental Habits

95. The interview was with Muireann Irish: Brancatisano, Emma. 2017. "Here's How Picking Up a New Skill Can Help Your Brain." Huffington Post, January 18, 2017, sec. Life. https://www.huffingtonpost.com.au/2017/01/18/heres-how-picking-up-a-new-skill-can-help-your-brain_a_21657171/.

96. The process of our brains' muscle-building: Doidge, Norman. 2015. *The Brain's Way of Healing: Remarkable Discoveries and Recoveries from the Frontiers of Neuroplasticity.* New York, NY: Viking.

96. New experiences cause neurons: Tang, Yi-Yuan. 2017. *The Neuroscience of Mindfulness Meditation: How the Body and Mind Work Together to Change Our Behaviour.* Palgrave.

Chapter 14: Meditation for Brain Fitness

100. Western medicines tend to: Rakel, David. 2012. *Integrative Medicine.* Philadelphia, PA: Saunders.

100. According to neuroscientist: Dispenza, Joe. 2015. *You Are the Placebo: Making Your Mind Matter.* Carlsbad, California: Hay House.

101. An important tip for beginners: Kornfield, Jack. 2010. *Meditation for Beginners.* Jaico Publishing House.

102. The most important consideration: Decker, Benjamin W. 2018. *Practical Meditation for Beginners: 10 Days to a Happier, Calmer You.* Emeryville, CA: Althea Press.

Chapter 15: The Power of the Self-Healing Breath

103. It's unfortunate because learned: Hendricks, Gay. 1995. *Conscious Breathing: Breathwork for Health, Stress Release, and Personal Mastery.* New York: Bantam Books.

104. Breathing techniques have been: Vranich, Belisa. 2020. *Breathing for Warriors: Master*

Your Breath to Unlock More Strength, Greater Endurance, Sharper Precision, Faster Recovery, and an Unshakable Inner Game. St. Martins.

104.   In addition, deep breathing: Rosenberg, Stanley, Benjamin Shield, and Stephen W Porges. 2017. *Accessing the Healing Power of the Vagus Nerve: Self-Help Exercises for Anxiety, Depression, Trauma, and Autism.* North Atlantic Books.

105.   Here's one of the easier breathing exercises: Bloch, Yael. 2019. *Breathe Slower, Deeper, Better: Make Deep Breathing a Habit With Simple Yoga Exercises.* New York: Workman Pub CO Inc.

Chapter 16: Do One Thing at a Time

109.   Where you direct it: Goleman, Daniel. 2013. *Focus: The Hidden Driver of Excellence.* New York: Harper.

110.   I thought that multitasking: Crenshaw, Dave. 2008. *The Myth of Multitasking: How "Doing It All" Gets Nothing Done.* San Francisco: Jossey-Bass.

111.   Now when I'm talking: Ruiz, Don Miguel. 1997. *The Four Agreements: A Practical Guide to Personal Freedom.* Amber-Allen Publishing.

111.   There's a wonderful ancient Zen: Zack, Devora. 2015. *Singletasking: Get More Done, One Thing at a Time.* Berrett-Koehler Publishers.

112.   If whatever you're doing: Tolle, Eckhart. 2008. *A New Earth: Awakening to Your Life's Purpose.* New York: Penguin.

112.   "Do one thing at a time": Allen, David. 2015. *Getting Things Done: The Art of Stress-Free Productivity.* Penguin Books.

Part Two Conclusion

115.   Our behavior and reactions: Murphy, Joseph. 2008. *The Power of Your Subconscious Mind.* New York: Wilder Pr.

116.   Our thoughts can break free: Singer, Michael A. 2007. *The Untethered Soul: The Journey Beyond Yourself.* Oakland, CA: New Harbinger Publications.

117.   Complex tasks keep the brain: Duhigg, Charles. 2012. *The Power of Habit: Why We Do What We Do in Life and Business.* New York: Random House.

PART THREE: THE EMOTIONAL ENERGY CENTER

120.   Our emotional energy center: Alcantara, Margarita. 2017. *Chakra Healing: A Beginner's Guide to Self-Healing Techniques That Balance the Chakras.* Berkeley, CA: Althea Press.

120.   There are a number: Frazier, Karen. 2019. *The Little Book of Energy Healing Techniques: Simple Practices to Heal Body, Mind, and Spirit.* Emeryville, California: Althea Press.

121.   Sit comfortably, back straight: Pfender, April. 2019. *Essential Chakra Meditation: Awaken Your Healing Power with Meditation and Visualization.* Althea Press.

121.   To emphasize the importance: Redmond, Layne. 2010. *Chakra Meditation: Transformation Through the Seven Energy Centers of the Body.* Sounds True.

123.   Every minute, with every heartbeat: Childre, Doc, Howard Martin, and Deborah Rozman. 2016. *Heart Intelligence: Connecting with the Intuitive Guidance of the Heart.* Cardiff, California: Waterfront Press.

Chapter 17: Your Heart Intelligence Is More Powerful Than Your Brain Intelligence

125.   A beautiful quote from: Hellstrom, Travis. 2016. *The Dalai Lama Book of Quotes: A Collection of Speeches, Quotations, Essays and Advice from His Holiness.* Hatherleigh Press.

126.   EQ is defined as: Goleman, Daniel. 2005. *Emotional Intelligence: 10th Anniversary Edition; Why It Can Matter More Than IQ,* Bantam.

126.   In fact, according to: Deutschendorf, Harvey. 2016. "7 Reasons Why Emotional Intelligence Is One of The Fastest-Growing Job Skills." Fast Company. Fast Company. May 4, 2016. https://www.fastcompany.com/3059481/7-reasons-why-emotional-intelligence-is-one-of-the-fastest-growing-job-skills.

126.   One of the institute's founders: Childre, Doc, Howard Martin, and Deborah Rozman.

2016. *Heart Intelligence: Connecting with the Intuitive Guidance of the Heart.* Cardiff, California: Waterfront Press.

127. Gregg Braden, best-selling author: Braden, Gregg. 2019. *The Science of Self-Empowerment: Awakening the New Human Story.* Hay House.

Chapter 18: Be Your Best Friend: Practical Ways to Enhance Your Resilience

129. We're trained from the time: Robbins, Alexandra. 2006. *The Overachievers: The Secret Lives of Driven Kids.* New York: Hachette.

130. A study published in: Ford, Brett Q., Phoebe Lam, Oliver P. John, and Iris B. Mauss. 2018. "The Psychological Health Benefits of Accepting Negative Emotions and Thoughts: Laboratory, Diary, and Longitudinal Evidence." *Journal of Personality and Social Psychology* 115 (6): 1075–92. https://doi.org/10.1037/pspp0000157.

130. Acknowledging negative emotions: David, Susan A. 2016. *Emotional Agility: Get Unstuck, Embrace Change, and Thrive in Work and Life.* New York: Avery.

131. There's a hormone called oxytocin: Lisa Feldman Barrett. 2017. *How Emotions Are Made: The Secret Life of the Brain.* Boston: Mariner Books.

132. Impermanence is inevitable: Brehm, John. 2017. *The Poetry of Impermanence, Mindfulness, and Joy.* Boston: Wisdom Publications.

133. There's a wonderful parable: Becker, Laney Katz. 2007. *Three Times Chai: 54 Rabbis Tell Their Favorite Stories.* Springfield, Nj: Behrman House.

Chapter 19: Forgiveness, Hawaiian Style

135. Ho'oponopono's literal translation: Bodin, Luc, Nathalie Bodin Lamboy, Jean Graciet, and Jon E Graham. 2016. *The Book of Ho'oponopono: The Hawaiian Practice of Forgiveness and Healing.* Rochester, Vermont: Destiny Books.

136. It's been refined by: Len, Ihaleakala Hew, Kamailelauli'I Rafaelovich, and Momilani Ramstrum. 2019. *Blue Ice: Self I-Dentity Through Ho'oponopono® Mskr SITH® Conversations, Book 5: How to Clean: How to Clean.* Bingboard Consulting. https://books.google.com/books/about/Blue_Ice.html?id=m1yUxgEACAAJ.

136. According to Hawaiian tradition: King, Serge Kahili. 2008. *Huna: Ancient Hawaiian Secrets for Modern Living.* New York: Atria Books.

Chapter 20: Letting Go of Emotional Pain: A Personal Story

139. People describe the effects: Kehr, Bruce Alan. 2018. *Becoming Whole: A Healing Companion to Ease Emotional Pain and Find Self-Love.* Austin, TX: Greenleaf Book Group.

140. I went through a period: Chödrön, Pema. 2016. *When Things Fall Apart: Heart Advice for Difficult Times.* Boulder, Colorado: Shambhala.

141. The most important thing: Daphne Rose Kingma. 2004. *Loving Yourself: Four Steps to a Happier You.* Boston, Ma: Conari Press.

142. From that indelible experience: Nh t H nh, Thích. 1998. *The Heart of the Buddha's Teaching: Transforming Suffering into Peace, Joy & Liberation: The Four Noble Truths, the Noble Eightfold Path, and Other Basic Buddhist Teachings.* Berkeley, Ca.: Parallax Press.

144. The way to thrive: Dalai Lama [Tenzin Gyatso] and Desmond Tutu. 2016. *The Book of Joy: Lasting Happiness in a Changing World.* With Douglas Abrams. New York: Avery.

144. I hope it will be: Gutsol, Olga. 2019. *108 Buddhist Parables and Stories.* Olga Produ.

Chapter 21: The Health of Our Planet: A Reflection of the Health of Our Modern Society

147. In 2019 the Intergovernmental: Bongaarts, John. 2019. "Summary for Policymakers of the Global Assessment Report on Biodiversity and Ecosystem Services of the Intergovernmental Science Policy Platform on Biodiversity and Ecosystem Services." *Population and Development Review* 45 (3): 680–81. https://doi.org/10.1111/padr.12283.

148   The speed at which: Wilson, Edward O. 2016. *Half-Earth: Our Planet's Fight For Life.* New York: Liveright Publishing Corporation.

150. We are as interconnected: Kimmerer, Robin Wall. 2020. *Braiding Sweetgrass Indigenous Wisdom, Scientific Knowledge and the Teachings of Plants.* Penguin Books.

150. "There is mounting evidence": Rodriguez, Tori. 2018. "The Mental Health Benefits of Nature Exposure - Psychiatry Advisor." Psychiatry Advisor. December 17, 2018. https://www.psychiatryadvisor.com/home/topics/mood-disorders/the-mental-health-benefits-of-nature-exposure/.

150. And according to Madhuleena: Chowdhury, Madhuleena Roy. 2019. "The Positive Effects of Nature on Your Mental Well-Being." Positive Psychology. July 4, 2019. https://positivepsychology.com/positive-effects-of-nature/.

150. The answer lies partially: Centers for Disease Control and Prevention. 2019a. "NVSS - Mortality Data." Centers for Disease Control and Prevention. 2019. https://www.cdc.gov/nchs/nvss/deaths.htm.

150. The Centers for Disease Control: Centers for Disease Control and Prevention. 2020. "Products - Data Briefs - Number 361 - March 2020." Centers for Disease Control and Prevention. April 7, 2020. https://www.cdc.gov/nchs/products/databriefs/db362.htm.

151. Unfortunately, in the busy-ness: Hallowell, Edward M. 2007. *CrazyBusy: Overstretched, Overbooked, and About to Snap! Strategies for Handling Your Fast-Paced Life.* New York: Ballantine Books.

152. The U.S. Department of Agriculture: U.S. Department of Agriculture. Ers.usda.gov. 2020. Available at: <https://www.ers.usda.gov/webdocs/publications/94849/err-270.pdf>.

152. A 2018 report from: Coleman-Jensen, Alisha, Mark Nord, Margaret Andrews, and Steven Carlson. 2011. "Household Food Security in the United States in 2010." *SSRN Electronic Journal.* https://doi.org/10.2139/ssrn.2116606.

152. A common practice called: Clover, Charles. 2008. *The End of the Line: How Overfishing Is Changing the World and What We Eat.* Berkeley: University of California Press.

152. "The Economist" reports that: The Economist. 2020. "The Global Food Supply Chain Is Passing a Severe Test." The Economist. May 9, 2020. https://www.economist.com/leaders/2020/05/09/the-global-food-supply-chain-is-passing-a-severe-test.

153. This growing appetite for meat: Jonathan Safran Foer. 2019. *We Are the Weather: Saving the Planet Begins at Breakfast.* New York: Farrar Straus and Giroux.

153. In this endless, materialistic sprint: Jahren, Hope. 2020. *The Story of More: How We Got to Climate Change and Where to Go from Here.* New York: Vintage Books.

154. "Being" reflects a life force: Brown, Brené. 2010. *The Gifts of Imperfection: Let Go of Who You Think You're Supposed to Be and Embrace Who You Are.* Center City, Minn.: Hazelden.

Conclusion: Your Limitless & Eternal Nature

157. We happen to be living: Furst, Dan. 2011. *Surfing Aquarius: How to Ace the Wave of Change.* San Francisco, CA: Red Wheel/Weiser.

158. The currently dawning of Aquarius: Woolfolk, Joanna Martine. 1999. *The Only Astrology Book You'll Ever Need.* Taylor Trade Publishing.

158. Ben Goertzel, CEO and: Sahota, Neil, and Michael Ashley. 2019. *Own the A.I. Revolution: Unlock Your Artificial Intelligence Strategy to Disrupt Your Competition.* New York: Mcgraw-Hill.

158. With molecular nanotechnologies: Tegmark, Max. 2017. *Life 3.0: Being Human In the Age of Artificial Intelligence.* New York: Knopf Publishing Group.

159. With a worldwide understanding: Kaku, Michio. 2019. *The Future of Humanity: Our Destiny In the Universe.* New York: Anchor Books.

160. According to researchers: Napier, Kathleen, and Lior Shamir. 2018. "Quantitative Sentiment Analysis of Lyrics in Popular Music." *Journal of Popular Music Studies* 30 (4): 161–76. https://doi.org/10.1525/jpms.2018.300411.

162. Throughout the history of humanity: Harari, Yuval N, John Purcell, and Haim Watzman. 2015. *Sapiens: A Brief History of Humankind.* New York: Harper.

164. The Ultimate Reality isn't happening: Chopra, Deepak. 2017. *You Are the Universe: Discovering Your Cosmic Self and Why It Matters.* Harmony.

Bibliography

Akimov, Aleksandr V, and Gennadij D Kazakevič. 2020. *30 Years Since the Fall of the Berlin Wall: Turns and Twists in Economies, Politics, and Societies in the Post-Communist Countries.* Singapore Palgrave Macmillan.

Alcantara, Margarita. 2017. *Chakra Healing: A Beginner's Guide to Self-Healing Techniques That Balance the Chakras.* Berkeley, CA: Althea Press.

Alisa Marie Fleming. 2018. *Go Dairy Free: The Ultimate Guide and Cookbook for Milk Allergies, Lactose Intolerance, and Casein-Free Living.* Dallas, TX: Benbella Books.

Allen, David. 2015. *Getting Things Done: The Art of Stress-Free Productivity.* Penguin Books.

Annibali, Joseph A. 2015. *Reclaim Your Brain: How to Calm Your Thoughts, Heal Your Mind, and Bring Your Life Back Under Control.* New York: Avery.

Aster. 2018. *Cacao Cookbook: Discover the Health Benefits and Uses of Cacao, With 50 Delicious Recipes.* London: Aster.

Avison, Joanne. 2015. *Yoga: Fascia, Form and Functional Movement.* Edinburgh: Handspring Publishing.

Barber, Susan. 2000. "Bioenergy Fields: The End of All Disease? With Valerie Hunt." The Spirit of Ma'at. November 2000. http://www.spiritofmaat.com/archive/nov1/vh.htm.

Bartholomew, Rachel, and Mandy Pearson. 2014. *Mindful Eating: Stop Mindless Eating and Learn to Nourish Body and Soul.* Cico.

Bauer, Joy. 2018. *Joy's Simple Food Remedies: Tasty Cures for Whatever's Ailing You.* Carlsbad, California: Hay House, Inc.

Becker, Adam. 2018. *What Is Real?: The Unfinished Quest For the Meaning of Quantum Physics.* New York, Ny: Basic Books.

Becker, Laney Katz. 2007. *Three Times Chai: 54 Rabbis Tell Their Favorite Stories.* Springfield, Nj: Behrman House.

Berger, Bethany. 2005. "Justice and the Outsider: Jurisdiction Over NonMembers in Tribal Legal Systems." *Faculty Articles and Papers, January.* https://opencommons.uconn.edu/law_papers/190.

Berson, Josh. 2019. *The Meat Question: Animals, Humans, and the Deep History of Food.* Random House.

Bloch, Yael. 2019. *Breathe Slower, Deeper, Better: Make Deep Breathing a Habit With Simple Yoga Exercises.* New York: Workman Pub CO Inc.

Bodin, Luc, Nathalie Bodin Lamboy, Jean Graciet, and Jon E Graham. 2016. *The Book of Ho'oponopono: The Hawaiian Practice of Forgiveness and Healing.* Rochester, Vermont: Destiny Books.

Bongaarts, John. 2019. "Summary for Policymakers of the Global Assessment Report on Biodiversity and Ecosystem Services of the Intergovernmental Science Policy Platform on Biodiversity and Ecosystem Services." *Population and Development Review* 45 (3): 680–81. https://doi.org/10.1111/padr.12283.

Boyers, Lindsay. 2019. *Intermittent Fasting Basics: Your Guide to the Essentials of Intermittent Fasting--And How It Can Work for You!* New York: Adams Media.

Braden, Gregg. 2019. *The Science of Self-Empowerment: Awakening the New Human Story.* Hay House.

Bramble, Ben, and Bob Fischer. 2016. *The Moral Complexities of Eating Meat.* New York, NY: Oxford University Press.

Brancatisano, Emma. 2017. "Here's How Picking Up a New Skill Can Help Your Brain." *Huffington Post,* January 18, 2017, sec. Life. https://www.huffingtonpost.com. au/2017/01/18/heres-how-picking-up-a-new-skill-can-help-your-brain_a_21657171/.

Brehm, John. 2017. *The Poetry of Impermanence, Mindfulness, and Joy.* Boston: Wisdom Publications.

Bremmer, Jan. 1987. *The Early Greek Concept of the Soul.* Princeton, N.J.: Princeton University Press, C.

Brown, Brené. 2010. *The Gifts of Imperfection: Let Go of Who You Think You're Supposed to Be and Embrace Who You Are.* Center City, Minn.: Hazelden.

Brown, Judith. 2016. *Nutrition Now.* Cengage Learning, Inc.

Buettner, Dan. 2015. *The Blue Zones Solution: Eating and Living Like the World's Healthiest People.* Hanover, PA: National Geographic Society.

Campbell, T. Colin. 2017. *The China Study: The Most Comprehensive Study of Nutrition Ever Conducted and the Startling Implications for Diet, Weight Loss and Long-Term Health.* Dallas, TX: Benbella Books, Inc.

Carpenter, Murray. 2015. *Caffeinated: How Our Daily Habit Helps, Hurts, and Hooks Us.* New York: Plume Books.

Carr, Allen. 2016. *Good Sugar Bad Sugar: Eat Yourself Free from Sugar and Carb Addiction.* London: Arcturus.

Carter, Rita, Susan Aldridge, Martyn Page, and Steve Parker. 2014. *The Human Brain Book: An Illustrated Guide to Its Structure, Function, and Disorders.* New York: DK.

Centers for Disease Control and Prevention. 2019a. "NVSS - Mortality Data." Centers for Disease Control and Prevention. 2019. https://www.cdc.gov/nchs/nvss/deaths.htm.

Centers for Disease Control and Prevention. 2019b. "Sleep and Sleep Disorders." Centers for Disease Control and Prevention. 2019. https://www.cdc.gov/sleep/index.html.

Centers for Disease Control and Prevention. 2020. "Products - Data Briefs - Number 361 - March 2020." Centers for Disease Control and Prevention. April 7, 2020. https://www.cdc.gov/ nchs/products/databriefs/db362.htm.

Childre, Doc, Howard Martin, and Deborah Rozman. 2016. *Heart Intelligence: Connecting with the Intuitive Guidance of the Heart.* Cardiff, California: Waterfront Press.

Chödrön, Pema. 2016. *When Things Fall Apart: Heart Advice for Difficult Times.* Boulder, Colorado: Shambhala.

Chopra, Deepak. 2017. *You Are the Universe: Discovering Your Cosmic Self and Why It Matters.* Harmony.

Chowdhury, Madhuleena Roy. 2019. "The Positive Effects of Nature on Your Mental Well-Being." Positive Psychology. July 4, 2019. https://positivepsychology.com/positive-effects-of-nature/.

Clover, Charles. 2008. *The End of the Line: How Overfishing Is Changing the World and What We Eat*. Berkeley: University Of California Press.

Coleman-Jensen, Alisha, Mark Nord, Margaret Andrews, and Steven Carlson. 2011. "Household Food Security in the United States in 2010." *SSRN Electronic Journal*. https://doi.org/10.2139/ssrn.2116606.

Crenshaw, Dave. 2008. *The Myth of Multitasking: How "Doing It All" Gets Nothing Done*. San Francisco: Jossey-Bass.

Dalai Lama [Tenzin Gyatso] and Desmond Tutu. 2016. *The Book of Joy: Lasting Happiness in a Changing World*. With Douglas Abrams. New York: Avery.

Daphne Rose Kingma. 2004. *Loving Yourself: Four Steps to a Happier You*. Boston, Ma: Conari Press.

David, Susan A. 2016. *Emotional Agility: Get Unstuck, Embrace Change, and Thrive In Work and Life*. New York: Avery.

De Graaf, John, David Wann, and Thomas H Naylor. 2014. *Affluenza: How Overconsumption Is Killing Us--And How to Fight Back*. San Francisco: Berrett-Koehler Publishers.

Deatsman, Colleen. 2006. *Energy for Life: Connect With the Source*. Woodbury, Minn.: Llewellyn Publications.

Decker, Benjamin W. 2018. *Practical Meditation for Beginners: 10 Days to a Happier, Calmer You*. Emeryville, CA: Althea Press.

Deutschendorf, Harvey. 2016. "7 Reasons Why Emotional Intelligence Is One of The Fastest-Growing Job Skills." Fast Company. Fast Company. May 4, 2016. https://www.fastcompany.com/3059481/7-reasons-why-emotional-intelligence-is-one-of-the-fastest-growing-job-skills.

Dispenza, Joe. 2015. *You Are the Placebo: Making Your Mind Matter*. Carlsbad, California: Hay House.

Doidge, Norman. 2015. *The Brain's Way of Healing: Remarkable Discoveries and Recoveries from the Frontiers of Neuroplasticity*. New York, NY: Viking.

Dosch, Hans Günter. 2008. *Beyond the Nanoworld: Quarks, Leptons, and Gauge Bosons*. Wellesley, Mass.: A K Peters.

Dry January. 2018. *Try Dry: The Official Guide to a Month Off Booze*. London: Square Peg.

Duhigg, Charles. 2012. *The Power of Habit: Why We Do What We Do In Life and Business*. New York: Random House.

Ely, John. 2000. *Yoga-Yajnavalkya*. Madras Ganesh & Co.

Engel, Jonathan. 2018. *Fat Nation: A History of Obesity in America*. Lanham, Maryland: Rowman & Littlefield.

Esposito, Jennifer. 2014. *Jennifer's Way: My Journey with Celiac Disease--What Doctors Don't Tell You and How You Can Learn to Live Again*. Boston: Da Capo Lifelong Books.

Ewen, Robert B. 1998. *Personality: A Topical Approach: Theories, Research, Major Controversies, and Emerging Findings*. Mahwah N.J.: L. Erlbaum.

Ffrench, Rebecca. 2016. *Whole Protein Vegetarian: Delicious Plant-Based Recipes with Essential Amino Acids For Health and Well-Being*. Woodstock, VT: Countryman Press.

Fields, R. Douglas. 2020. *Electric Brain: How the New Science of Brainwaves Reads Minds, Tells Us How We Learn, and Helps Us Change for the Better.* Dallas, TX: Benbella Books, Inc.

Fiske, John. 1902. *The Miscellaneous Writings of John Fiske.* Boston: Houghton Mifflin.

Ford, Brett Q., Phoebe Lam, Oliver P. John, and Iris B. Mauss. 2018. "The Psychological Health Benefits of Accepting Negative Emotions and Thoughts: Laboratory, Diary, and Longitudinal Evidence." *Journal of Personality and Social Psychology* 115 (6): 1075–92. https://doi.org/10.1037/ pspp0000157.

Foster, Kelli C. 2020. *The Probiotic Kitchen: More Than 100 Delectable, Natural, and Supplement-Free Probiotic Recipes - Also Includes Recipes for Prebiotic Foods.* Beverly, MA: Harvard Common Press.

Frazier, Karen. 2019. *The Little Book of Energy Healing Techniques: Simple Practices to Heal Body, Mind, and Spirit.* Emeryville, California: Althea Press.

Furst, Dan. 2011. *Surfing Aquarius: How to Ace the Wave of Change.* San Francisco, CA: Red Wheel/Weiser.

Gershon, Michael D. 1999. *The Second Brain: The Scientific Basis of Gut Instinct & a Groundbreaking New Understanding of Nervous Disorders of the Stomach & Intestine.* New York: Harpercollins Publishers.

Gillespie, David. 2019. *The Good Fat Guide.* Sydney, N.S.W.: Pan Macmillan Australia.

Gladstar, Rosemary. 2008. *Rosemary Gladstar's Herbal Recipes for Vibrant Health: 175 Teas, Tonics, Oils, Salves, Tinctures, and Other Natural Remedies for the Entire Family.* North Adams, MA: Storey Pub.

Goleman, Daniel. 2005. *Emotional Intelligence: 10th Anniversary Edition; Why It Can Matter More Than IQ.* Bantam.

Goleman, Daniel. 2013. *Focus: The Hidden Driver of Excellence.* New York: Harper.

Goleman, Daniel, and Richard J Davidson. 2017. *Altered Traits: Science Reveals How Meditation Changes Your Mind, Brain, and Body.* Avery.

Goleman, Daniel. 2018. *The Science of Meditation: How to Change Your Brain, Mind and Body.* London, England: Penguin Life.

Gonzalez, Nicholas J. 2017. *Nutrition and the Autonomic Nervous System: The Scientific Foundations of the Gonzalez Protocol.* New York: New Spring Press.

Grace, Annie. 2018. *This Naked Mind: Control Alcohol, Find Freedom, Discover Happiness & Change Your Life.* New York: Avery.

Guo, Bisong, and Andrew Powell. 2001. *Listen to Your Body: The Wisdom of the Dao.* Honolulu: University of Hawaii Press.

Gurtner, Karin, and Thomas W Myers. 2019. *Anatomy Trains in Motion: Embrain and Embody Myofascial Meridian Anatomy.* Independently Published.

Gutsol, Olga. 2019. *108 Buddhist Parables and Stories.* Olga Produ.

Hallowell, Edward M. 2007. *CrazyBusy: Overstretched, Overbooked, and About to Snap! Strategies For Handling Your Fast-Paced Life.* New York: Ballantine Books.

Hanson, Rick, and Richard Mendius. 2009. *Buddha's Brain: The Practical Neuroscience of Happiness, Love, and Wisdom*. Oakland, CA: New Harbinger Publications.

Harari, Yuval N, John Purcell, and Haim Watzman. 2015. *Sapiens: A Brief History of Humankind*. New York: Harper.

Harris, Ryan. 2019. *Neuroplasticity: A Complete Guide to Neuroplasticity Techniques & Practices to Improve Your Brain Function, Develop New Ways of Thinking & Create New Approaches to Life & Relationships*. Kontakt Digital.

Harvey, Andrew. 1999. *Teachings of Rumi*. Boston: Shambhala.

Hellstrom, Travis. 2016. *The Dalai Lama Book of Quotes: A Collection of Speeches, Quotations, Essays and Advice from His Holiness*. Hatherleigh Press.

Hendricks, Gay. 1995. *Conscious Breathing: Breathwork for Health, Stress Release, and Personal Mastery*. New York: Bantam Books.

Hergenhahn, B. R. 2009. *An Introduction to the History of Psychology*. Wadsworth Publishing.

Hippocrates, J Chadwick, G E R Lloyd, and W N Mann. 1984. *Hippocratic Writings*. Penguin.

Hunter, MaryCarol R., Brenda W. Gillespie, and Sophie Yu-Pu Chen. 2019. "Urban Nature Experiences Reduce Stress in the Context of Daily Life Based on Salivary Biomarkers." *Frontiers in Psychology* 10 (April). https://doi.org/10.3389/fpsyg.2019.00722.

Jahren, Hope. 2020. *The Story of More: How We Got to Climate Change and Where to Go from Here*. New York: Vintage Books.

Jernigan, David. 2017. "Global Developments in Alcohol Policies: Progress in Implementation of the WHO Global Strategy to Reduce the Harmful Use of Alcohol since 2010." https://www.who.int/substance_abuse/activities/fadab/msb_adab_gas_progress_report.pdf?ua=1.

Johnson, Rebecca L. 2012. *Your Digestive System*. Lerner Classroom.

Jonathan Safran Foer. 2019. *We Are the Weather: Saving the Planet Begins at Breakfast*. New York: Farrar Straus and Giroux.

Kabat-Zinn, Jon. 2013. *Full Catastrophe Living: Using the Wisdom of Your Body and Mind to Face Stress, Pain, and Illness*. New York: Bantam Books.

Kaku, Michio. 2019. *The Future of Humanity: Our Destiny in the Universe*. New York: Anchor Books.

Kehr, Bruce Alan. 2018. *Becoming Whole: A Healing Companion to Ease Emotional Pain and Find Self-Love*. Austin, TX: Greenleaf Book Group.

Kimmerer, Robin Wall. 2020. *Braiding Sweetgrass Indigenous Wisdom, Scientific Knowledge and the Teachings of Plants*. Penguin Books.

King, Serge Kahili. 2008. *Huna: Ancient Hawaiian Secrets for Modern Living*. New York: Atria Books.

King, Vex. 2018. *Good Vibes, Good Life: How Self-Love Is the Key to Unlocking Your Greatness*. Carlsbad, California: Hay House.

Klotsche, Charles. 1994. *Color Medicine: The Secrets of Color Vibrational Healing*. Sedona, AZ: Light Technology Pub.

Knight, Rob, and Brendan Buhler. 2015. *Follow Your Gut: The Enormous Impact of Tiny Microbes.* New York: Simon & Schuster/TED.

Kornfield, Jack. 2010. *Meditation for Beginners.* Jaico Pub. House.

Kresser, Chris. 2014. *The Paleo Cure: Eat Right for Your Genes, Body Type, and Personal Health Needs -- Prevent and Reverse Disease, Lose Weight Effortlessly, and Look and Feel Better Than Ever.* New York: Little, Brown Spark.

Larkam, Elizabeth J. 2017. *Fascia in Motion: Fascia-Focused Movement For Pilates.* Edinburgh: Handspring Publishing.

Lasater, Judith. 2015. *Living Your Yoga: Finding the Spiritual In Everyday Life.* Berkeley, California: Rodmell Press.

Lefae, Phoenix. 2019. *What Is Remembered Lives: Developing Relationships with Deities, Ancestors & the Fae.* Woodbury, MN: Llewellyn Publications.

Leitenbauer, Hubert. 2014. *Prana Energy-Therapy: A NON-CONTACT METHOD OF HEALING.* Freya. https://www.amazon.com/dp/B00RZMWYXC.

Len, Ihaleakala Hew, Kamailelauli'I Rafaelovich, and Momilani Ramstrum. 2019. *Blue Ice: Self I-Dentity Through Ho'oponopono® Mskr SITH® Conversations, Book 5: How to Clean: How to Clean.* Bingboard Consulting. https://books.google.com/books/about/Blue_Ice.html?id=m1yUxgEACAAJ.

Levinovitz, Alan. 2015. *The Gluten Lie: And Other Myths About What You Eat.* New York: Regan Arts.

Li, Qing. 2018. *Forest Bathing: How Trees Can Help You Find Health and Happiness.* New York, NY: Viking.

Li, William W. 2019. *Eat to Beat Disease: The New Science of How Your Body Can Heal Itself.* New York: Grand Central Publishing.

Lisa Feldman Barrett. 2017. *How Emotions Are Made: The Secret Life of the Brain.* Boston: Mariner Books.

Madiyev, Oybek. 2020. "Uzbekistan's International Relations," June. https://doi.org/10.4324/9780429327629.

Maitland, Jeffrey. 2016. *Embodied Being: The Philosophical Roots of Manual Therapy.* North Atlantic Books.

Mayer, Emeran A. 2018. *The Mind-Gut Connection: How the Hidden Conversation Within Our Bodies Impacts Our Mood, Our Choices, and Our Overall Health.* Harper Wave.

Mcclelland, Norman C. 2010. *Encyclopedia of Reincarnation and Karma.* Mcfarland & Company.

Mclaren, Karla. 1998. *Your Aura & Your Chakras: The Owner's Manual.* Weiser Books.

Morris, Joshua. 2013. *Acorns: Windows High-Tide Foghat: Volume III.* iUniverse. https://www.amazon.com/dp/B079J4TR8B/.

Muller, Divo, and Karin Hertzer. 2017. *Train Your Fascia Tone Your Body: The Successful Method to Form Firm Connective Tissue.* Meyer & Meyer Media.

Murphy, Joseph. 2008. *The Power of Your Subconscious Mind.* New York: Wilder Pr.

Myss, Caroline. 1997. *Anatomy of the Spirit: The Seven Stages of Power and Healing.* New York, New York: Harmony.

Napier, Kathleen, and Lior Shamir. 2018. "Quantitative Sentiment Analysis of Lyrics in Popular Music." *Journal of Popular Music Studies* 30 (4): 161–76. https://doi.org/10.1525/jpms.2018.300411.

New Scientist. 2017. *Your Conscious Mind: Unravelling the Greatest Mystery of the Human Brain.* Boston, MA: Nicholas Brealey Publishing.

Nh t H nh, Thích. 1998. *The Heart of the Buddha's Teaching: Transforming Suffering Into Peace, Joy & Liberation: The Four Noble Truths, the Noble Eightfold Path, and Other Basic Buddhist Teachings.* Berkeley, Ca.: Parallax Press.

Ni, Mao Shing. 2008. *Secrets of Self-Healing: Harness Nature's Power to Heal Common Ailments, Boost Your Vitality, and Achieve Optimum Wellness.* New York, NY: Avery.

Ober, Clinton. 2014. *Earthing: The Most Important Health Discovery Ever!* Basic Health Publications.

Openshaw, Robyn. 2017. *Vibe: Unlock the Energetic Frequencies of Limitless Health, Love & Success.* Gallery Books.

Paarlberg, Robert L. 2015. *The United States of Excess: Gluttony and the Dark Side of American Exceptionalism.* Oxford University Press.

Parker, Steve, and Robert M L Winston. 2007. *The Human Body Book.* New York: DK Publishing.

Peirce, Penney. 2011. *Frequency: The Power of Personal Vibration.* New York: Atria Books.

Perlov, Delia, and Alex Vilenkin. 2018. *Cosmology for the Curious.* Springer.

Pfender, April. 2019. *Essential Chakra Meditation: Awaken Your Healing Power with Meditation and Visualization.* Althea Press.

Rakel, David. 2012. *Integrative Medicine.* Philadelphia, PA: Saunders.

Redmond, Layne. 2010. *Chakra Meditation: Transformation Through the Seven Energy Centers of the Body.* Sounds True.

Reinhard, Tonia. 2014. *Superfoods: The Healthiest Foods on the Planet.* Buffalo, NY: Firefly Books.

Robbins, Alexandra. 2006. *The Overachievers: The Secret Lives of Driven Kids.* New York: Hachette.

Rodin, Kathleen. 2018. *Reboot: Release Emotions and Remember Wholeness Using Essential Oils.* Oily Baalievers Publishing.

Rodriguez, Tori. 2018. "The Mental Health Benefits of Nature Exposure - Psychiatry Advisor." Psychiatry Advisor. December 17, 2018. https://www.psychiatryadvisor.com/home/topics/mood-disorders/the-mental-health-benefits-of-nature-exposure/.

Romeo, Elisa. 2015. *Meet Your Soul: A Powerful Guide to Connect with Your Most Sacred Self.* Hay House.

Rosenberg, Stanley, Benjamin Shield, and Stephen W Porges. 2017. *Accessing the Healing Power of the Vagus Nerve: Self-Help Exercises for Anxiety, Depression, Trauma, and Autism.* North Atlantic Books.

Ruiz, Don Miguel. 1997. *The Four Agreements: A Practical Guide to Personal Freedom.* Amber-Allen Publishing.

Rutkowski, Anne-Françoise, and Carol S Saunders. 2018. *Emotional and Cognitive Overload: The Dark Side of Information Technology.* Routledge.

Ryan, Christopher. 2019. *Civilized to Death: The Price of Progress.* New York: Avid Reader Press.

Sabaté, Joan. 2019. *Environmental Nutrition: Connecting Health and Nutrition with Environmentally Sustainable Diets.* Academic.

Sahota, Neil, and Michael Ashley. 2019. *Own the A.I. Revolution: Unlock Your Artificial Intelligence Strategy to Disrupt Your Competition.* New York: Mcgraw-Hill.

Schulte, Erica M., Nicole M. Avena, and Ashley N. Gearhardt. 2015. "Which Foods May Be Addictive? The Roles of Processing, Fat Content, and Glycemic Load." Edited by Tiffany L. Weir. *PLOS ONE* 10 (2): e0117959. https://doi.org/10.1371/journal.pone.0117959.

Seaward, Brian Luke. 2012. *Health of the Human Spirit: Spiritual Dimensions for Personal Health.* ones & Bartlett Publishers.

Shelton, Will. 2017. *Investing in Your Health... You'll Love the Returns.* First Edition Design Publishing.

Shewfelt, Robert L. 2016. *In Defense of Processed Food: It's Not Nearly As Bad As You Think.* Copernicus Books.

Shumsky, Susan. 2013. *Power of Auras: Tap into Your Energy Field for Clarity, Peace of Mind, and Well-Being.* New Page Books.

Siegel, Daniel J, and Marion Fried Solomon. 2020. *Mind, Consciousness, and Well-Being.* New York: W. W. Norton & Company.

Singer, Michael A. 2007. *The Untethered Soul: The Journey Beyond Yourself.* Oakland, CA: New Harbinger Publications.

Skinner, Stephen. 2009. *Sacred Geometry: Deciphering the Code.* New York: Sterling.

Spear, Susan E. 2017. *Mission Nutrition: Calories Matter but They Don't Count... at Least Not the Way You Think They Do.* Gilbert, AZ: Nutrutious Insight.

Stephen Snehan Cherniske. 2008. *Caffeine Blues Wake up to the Hidden Dangers of America's #1 Drug.* Boston: Grand Central Publishing.

Stossel, Scott. 2015. *My Age of Anxiety: Fear, Hope, Dread, and the Search for Peace of Mind.* New York: Vintage.

Tang, Yi-Yuan. 2017. *The Neuroscience of Mindfulness Meditation: How the Body and Mind Work Together to Change Our Behaviour.* Palgrave.

Taubes, Gary. 2017. *The Case Against Sugar.* New York: Anchor Books.

Tegmark, Max. 2017. Life 3.0: *Being Human In the Age of Artificial Intelligence.* New York: Knopf Publishing Group.

Temple, Nicola. 2018. *Best Before: The Evolution and Future of Processed Food.* Bloomsbury Sigma.

The Economist. 2020. "The Global Food Supply Chain Is Passing a Severe Test." The Economist. May 9, 2020. https://www.economist.com/leaders/2020/05/09/the-global-food-supply-chain-is-passing-a-severe-test.

Thompson, Evan. 2015. *Waking, Dreaming, Being: Self and Consciousness in Neuroscience, Meditation, and Philosophy.* New York: Columbia University Press.

Tolle, Eckhart. 2004. *The Power of Now: A Guide to Spiritual Enlightenment.* New World Library.

Tolle, Eckhart. 2008. *A New Earth: Awakening to Your Life's Purpose.* New York: Penguin.

Vasey, Christopher. 2014. *Natural Remedies for Inflammation.* Rochester, Vermont: Healing Arts Press.

Vranich, Belisa. 2020. *Breathing for Warriors: Master Your Breath to Unlock More Strength, Greater Endurance, Sharper Precision, Faster Recovery, and an Unshakable Inner Game.* St. Martins.

Walker, Matthew. 2017. *Why We Sleep: Unlocking the Power of Sleep and Dream.* Scribner Book Company.

Ward, Peter D. 2015. *A New History of Life: The Radical New Discoveries About the Origins and Evolution of Life on Earth.* New York, NY: Bloomsbury Publishing.

Warner, Melanie. 2013. *Pandora's Lunchbox: How Processed Food Took Over the American Meal.* New York: Scribner Book Company.

Warrington, Ruby. 2019. *Sober Curious: The Blissful Sleep, Greater Focus, Limitless Presence, and Deep Connection Awaiting Us All on the Other Side of Alcohol.* New York, NY: Harperone.

Waxman, Denny, and Susan Waxman. 2015. *The Complete Macrobiotic Diet.* New York: Pegasus Books.

Weiss, Brian L. 1988. *Many Lives, Many Masters: The True Story of a Prominent Psychiatrist, His Young Patient, and the Past-Life Therapy That Changed Both Their Lives.* New York: Touchstone Books.

Wilson, Edward O. 2016. *Half-Earth: Our Planet's Fight for Life.* New York: Liveright Publishing Corporation.

Winters, Nasha, and Jess Higgins Kelley. 2017. The Metabolic Approach to Cancer: Integrating Deep Nutrition, the Ketogenic Diet, and Nontoxic Bio-Individualized Therapies. White River Junction, Vermont: Chelsea Green Publishing.

Wissler, Virginia. 2012. *Illuminated Pixels: The Why, What, and How of Digital Lighting.* Cengage Learning.

Woolfolk, Joanna Martine. 1999. *The Only Astrology Book You'll Ever Need.* Taylor Trade Publishing.

Wu, Zhongxian. 2011. *Chinese Shamanic Cosmic Orbit Qigong: Esoteric Talismans, Mantras, and Mudras in Healing and Inner Cultivation.* Singing Dragon.

Yafa, Stephen H. 2015. *Grain of Truth: The Real Case for and against Wheat and Gluten.* New York, NY: Avery.

Young, Rosamund. 2020. *The Secret Life of Cows.* Penguin Books.

Zack, Devora. 2015. *Singletasking: Get More Done, One Thing at a Time.* Berrett-Koehler Publishers.

"The current environment has placed huge strains on our society, and Lola's book can be a guiding light that brings solace and inner peace for the reader. While we live in uncertain times, it is important to maintain composure and balance in our lives— this can best be achieved by harnessing the positive energies of the mind, body and soul. Lola's book offers all that and a lot more - it provides valuable advice and guidance to reduce stress and improve general well-being. Mindfulness provides a stimulus of life, and can make you confident and productive, which in turn can positively influence how we interact with others. The book is a tonic we all need and a must read!"

Amir Dossal
President, Global Partnerships Forum

"As the author Lola Till states, many great thinkers have tried to answer life's great questions, using different knowledge bases to come to a range of answers. Here she uses an integrative approach, taking knowledge from science, philosophy, and spirituality to find the answers that help her achieve health, purpose, and contentment. This journey is one everyone should take for themselves, and this book can serve as a roadmap for people to find their own answers to life's essential questions."

Brian Kennedy
PhD, director of the Centre for Healthy Ageing, professor, departments of biochemistry and physiology, Yong Loo Lin School of Medicine, National University Singapore

"Immersed in the overall excellence of health and fascination of the power of mind and spirit, *Be Your Own Harmonist* helps you realize your full potential of self-mastery. Lola Till has succeeded in showing a course to reach higher levels of fulfillment and consciousness, perhaps even leading to hierophany and the release of the spiritual strength that exists within each and every one of us."

Evie Evangelou
Founder and president, Fashion 4 Development

"In trying times, the default reaction for most executives is to turn outward to face the challenge. Lola's book reminds us to turn inward, too. We are told regularly by environmentalists that we won't have any businesses to run if we destroy the natural resources around us. Likewise, our bodies will cease to function if we don't care for our diet, sleep, and mental health. *Be Your Own Harmonist* reminds us of the importance of self-care, and that to be an effective leader, you first need to feel it inside. After all, If you can't exercise control over your own body and mind, then what hope can you have of leading others?"

Grant Schreiber
Founding editor, *Real Leaders*

About the Author

Lola Till is the creator of The Harmonist Maison de Parfum and author of *Be Your Own Harmonist*. She holds a master's degree in international law, a doctorate degree in psychology, and an apprenticeship at the Gaia School of Herbal Medicine and Earth Education. She has dedicated herself to advancing knowledge and educating others about the delicate interplay between our physical, emotional, and mental health. As a businesswoman, philanthropist, and chairwoman of charitable foundations, as well as a mother of three, self-inquiry has been a driving force behind her research.

Made in the USA
Columbia, SC
06 September 2020

18469042R00129